DESSERTS

OVER 150 DELICIOUS IDEAS

DESSERTS

OVER 150 DELICIOUS IDEAS

LONGMEADOW
PRESS

Published by Longmeadow Press, 201 High Ridge Road,
Stamford, CT 06904.

ISBN: 0-681-45461-X

CREDITS

Contributing authors: Janice Murfitt, Mary Norwak and Sally Taylor
Photographers: David Gill, Paul Grater and Jan Stewart
Typeset by: The Old Mill, London
Color separation by: Scantrans Pte Ltd., Singapore

Printed in Italy

First Longmeadow Press Edition

0 9 8 7 6 5 4 3 2 1

Contents

Introduction

There can be no doubt about desserts—they are the crowning glory of a meal; the final expression of the thought and care you have taken in preparation and cooking. Whether you serve a homely Bread & Fruit Pudding or an exotic Choc Chestnut Gâteau, you can be sure that it will be greeted with delight by all at the table.

There are desserts for everybody and every season in this delicious collection. Such all-time favorites as Queen of Puddings, Pancakes, Oeufs à Neige and Strawberry Yogurt Molds will bring a smile to the faces of all children, and many a grown-up too! For an elegant lunch or dinner party, choose from such classics as Crème Brûlée, Charlotte Russe, Dacquoise or Hot Chocolate Soufflé, or delight your guests with something a little more unusual such as Framboise Zabaglione or Pink Grapefruit Cheesecake.

Many of the desserts in this book are extremely economical as well as quick and easy to make, while others, for those special occasions, require a little more time and costly ingredients. You can really let your imagination run riot decorating desserts: many of the quick desserts can be turned into party puddings simply by decorating them with rosettes of whipped cream, crystalized fruits, sugar flowers or edible flowers from the garden. Or lift an everyday pudding into the realms of the special by serving it with one of the delicious sauces from the chapter of sauces and accompaniments.

Points for Perfect Desserts

Remember these few key points when planning a dessert, particularly for a special occasion

- Serve a delicate dessert after a substantial starter and main course; if you wish to serve a hearty sweet course, keep the preceding courses light.
- Consider the textures in the meal and include crisp foods to contrast with soft or creamy dishes. Serve crisp biscuits with smooth desserts.
- Refreshing citrus desserts and ices follow spicy foods well.
- Plan a simple, prepare-ahead dessert if you are concentrating on last-minute dishes for the first part of the meal.
- If you intend serving a spectacular baked soufflé or similar sweet course which requires undivided last-minute attention, then prepare all the ingredients, utensils and cooking containers in advance. Prepare the recipe as far as possible beforehand.
- It is quite usual to offer a choice of desserts for a dinner party. In this case select two quite different dishes, often including one very light dessert as an alternative to a rich confection.
- Lastly, remember to warn guests not to overindulge in the savory courses if you have a spectacular and filling concoction making an entry at the end of the meal.

CREAMS, CUSTARDS
& DAIRY DESSERTS

Crunchy Maraschino Peaches

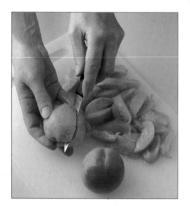

6 medium-size peaches
1/4 cup maraschino or other cherry liqueur
1-1/4 cups whipping cream
1/3 cup packed light-brown sugar
Fresh sweet cherries and leaves to garnish, if
    desired

Blanch peaches in boiling water 1 minute. Drain and peel. Cut pulp in thick slices. Discard pits.

Place peach slices in an oval flameproof dish, filling dish evenly. Pour liqueur over peaches. In a bowl, whip cream until stiff and drop spoonfuls on top of peaches. Gently spread whipped cream evenly. Cover dish with plastic wrap and refrigerate at least 4 hours.

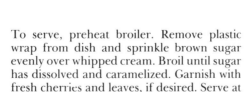

To serve, preheat broiler. Remove plastic wrap from dish and sprinkle brown sugar evenly over whipped cream. Broil until sugar has dissolved and caramelized. Garnish with fresh cherries and leaves, if desired. Serve at once.

Makes 6 servings.

Pineapple Mousse

2 large slices fresh pineapple
1(14-oz) can evaporated milk, well chilled
2/3 (1/4-oz.) envelope unflavored gelatin
    (2 teaspoons)
Juice of 1/2 lemon
Superfine sugar to taste
Crystalized pineapple and angelica leaves to
    decorate

Peel pineapple, removing eyes, and core. Puree pulp in a blender or food processor. In a small saucepan, bring pineapple puree to a boil and chill.

In a bowl, whip evaporated milk until thick and creamy. In a small bowl, sprinkle gelatin over lemon juice and let stand 2 to 3 minutes, until softened. Set bowl of gelatin in a saucepan of hot water and stir until dissolved. Stir into whipped milk.

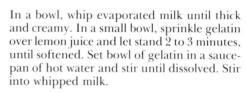

Fold pineapple puree into whipped milk and sweeten with sugar. Pour into a glass serving bowl or individual dessert dishes and chill until set. Decorate with crystallized pineapple and angelica leaves before serving.

Makes 4 servings.

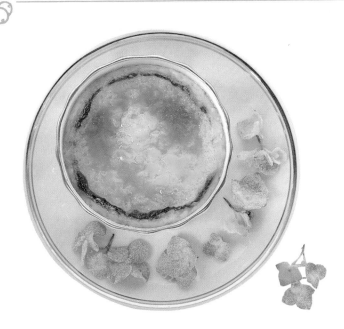

Crème Brûlée

4 egg yolks
2-1/2 teaspoons superfine sugar
Pinch of cornstarch
2-1/2 cups whipping cream
2 vanilla beans
Additional superfine sugar
Frosted flowers to serve, if desired

In a large bowl, beat egg yolks, sugar and cornstarch lightly.

Pour whipping cream into a saucepan. With a sharp knife, split open vanilla beans and scrape seeds into whipping cream. Bring almost to boiling point, strain and pour over yolks, beating constantly. Pour into top of a double boiler or a bowl set over a pan of simmering water. Cook over medium heat until mixture thickens sufficiently to coat back of a spoon. Pour into individual flameproof gratin dishes. Cool and chill overnight.

Two hours before serving, preheat broiler. Cover surface of pudding thickly and evenly with additional sugar and broil until sugar caramelizes. Chill 2 hours. Serve with frosted flowers, if desired.

Makes 4 to 6 servings.

NOTE: The best vanilla beans are coated in white crystals and are very expensive. All vanilla beans can be washed after use and used again. Store in a dry place.

Tropical Flummery

1-1/4 cups whipping cream
1/3 cup thawed frozen concentrated tropical fruit juice
1 egg white
1 tablespoon plus 2 teaspoons superfine sugar
Orange wedges and passion fruit to decorate, if desired
Langue de chats cookies to serve

In a bowl, whip cream to soft peaks.

Add fruit juice gradually, continuing to whip cream until fairly thick.

In a separate bowl, whisk egg white until stiff. Whisk in sugar, then fold into creamy mixture. Spoon into individual dessert dishes and chill 1 hour. Decorate with orange wedges and passion fruit, if desired. Serve with cookies.

Makes 4 to 6 servings,

NOTE: To flavor sugar for desserts and cakes, keep it in a container with a vanilla bean. This will give it a strong vanilla flavor.

Tipsy Fruit Fool

1 lb. cooking apples, peeled, sliced
1-1/4 cups dried apricots, pre-soaked
1/4 cup superfine sugar
Peel and juice 3 satsumas
2 tablespoons apricot brandy
1/3 cup fromage frais
Chocolate curls to decorate

In a saucepan, combine apples, apricots, sugar and satsuma peel and juice. Bring to a boil. Cover and cook until apples and apricots are tender. Remove satsuma peel and reserve some for decoration. Let stand until cold.

In a food processor fitted with a metal blade, process apple mixture to a purée. Add apricot brandy and fromage frais and process until well blended. Divide mixture among individual glasses and chill until needed.

Using a sharp knife, cut reserved peel in thin strips. Decorate desserts with satsuma peel strips and chocolate curls. Makes 6 servings.

Framboise Zabaglione

4 egg yolks
3/4 cup plus 2 tablespoons framboise liqueur
1 tablespoon plus 2 teaspoons superfine sugar
Fresh strawberries and leaves to garnish, if desired
Langue de chats cookies to serve

Combine egg yolks, liqueur and sugar in a double boiler or a bowl set over a pan of simmering water.

Whisk mixture over medium heat until very thick and mousse-like, about 20 minutes.

Pour mixture into serving dishes. Garnish with strawberries and leaves, if desired, and serve immediately with cookies.

Makes 4 servings.

NOTE: It is important to use a whisk for this recipe. An electric mixer increases the volume of the eggs too quickly so that they do not have a chance to cook. The mixture will then collapse when poured into the serving dishes.

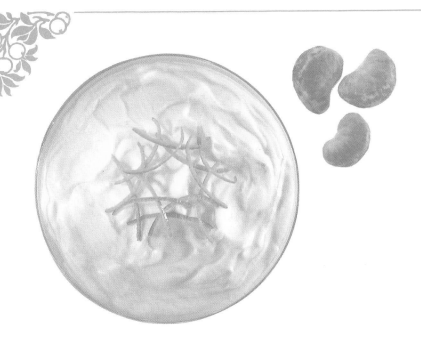

Tangerine Syllabub

Grated peel and juice of 3 tangerines
Grated peel and juice of 1 lemon
1/3 cup superfine sugar
1/3 cup cream sherry
1-1/4 cups whipping cream
Additional grated peel to decorate, if desired

In a bowl, combine tangerine and lemon peels and juices, sugar and sherry. Chill at least 1 hour to infuse.

In a large bowl, whip cream while gradually pouring in tangerine mixture. Whip until mixture is thick enough to form soft peaks.

Pour mixture into a glass serving bowl or individual dessert dishes and chill at least 2 hours before serving. Decorate with additional grated peel, if desired.

Makes 4 to 6 servings.

NOTE: Use a sharp grater to grate tangerine peel, otherwise peel tends to tear.
Warm citrus fruits slightly before squeezing and they will yield more juice.

Vanilla Bavarois

1-1/2 cups milk
1 vanilla bean or 3 drops vanilla extract
3 egg yolks
1 tablespoon plus 2 teaspoons superfine sugar
1 (1/4-oz) envelope unflavored gelatin
   (1 tablespoon)
1 tablespoon plus 2 teaspoons water
Grated nutmeg, if desired
3/4 cup whipping cream
1 recipe Black Currant & Cassis Sauce, page 90, or Dark Chocolate Sauce, page 92, to serve
Chocolate curls to decorate, if desired

In a saucepan, bring milk and vanilla bean or extract almost to boiling point. Remove from heat. Discard vanilla bean, if using.

In a bowl, beat egg yolks and sugar until thick and mousse-like. Pour hot milk onto mixture, beating constantly. Return to saucepan, set over low heat and stir until mixture thickens sufficiently to coat back of a spoon. Set aside. In a small bowl, sprinkle gelatin over water and let stand 2 to 3 minutes, until softened. Set bowl of gelatin in a saucepan of hot water and stir until dissolved. Add to milk mixture, stirring well. Chill until cool, stirring occasionally. Meanwhile, lightly oil a 3-3/4-cup mold.

When mixture is at setting point, add grated nutmeg, if desired. Whip cream lightly and fold into mixture. Spoon into oiled mold and refrigerate until set. Meanwhile, prepare Black Currant & Cassis Sauce or Dark Chocolate Sauce as directed. Turn out dessert and serve with sauce. Decorate with chocolate curls, if desired.

Makes 4 to 6 servings.

Rose Cream

2-1/2 cups whipping cream
1 (1/4-oz.) envelope unflavored gelatin
   (1 tablespoon)
2 tablespoons triple strength rose water
Grated peel and juice of 1 lemon
1/4 cup superfine sugar

Rose Petals:
1 egg white
Petals from 1 rose
Superfine sugar

To prepare rose petals, preheat oven to 225F (105C). Line a baking sheet with parchment paper. Whisk egg white until frothy and dip in rose petals to cover.

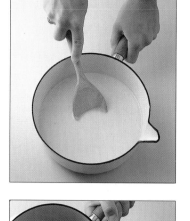

Toss dipped petals in sugar and place on prepared baking sheet. Place on bottom shelf of oven and bake about 2-1/2 hours, leaving oven door slightly ajar, until dry and hard. Store in an airtight container. Combine all ingredients for rose cream in a heavy-bottom saucepan and stir over very low heat until gelatin and sugar dissolve; do not boil.

Pour into 6 ramekin dishes and cool at room temperature. Refrigerate creams until ready to serve. Decorate with rose petals.

Makes 6 servings.

NOTE: Triple strength rose water is available from specialty food stores. The delicate flavor of ordinary rose water would be completely lost in this pudding.

Decorate with frosted rose leaves, if desired; do not eat frosted leaves.

Creamy Cranberry Fool

1/2 (12-oz.) package fresh cranberries
1/3 cup orange juice
3/4 cup superfine sugar
1-1/4 cups whipping cream
Grated orange peel, additional fresh
   cranberries and fresh leaves to decorate, if
   desired

In a saucepan, combine cranberries, orange juice and sugar. Simmer about 10 minutes, until berries pop; cool.

When cranberries are cold, using a wooden spoon, press through a fine metal sieve. In a large bowl, whip cream until stiff and fold in cranberry puree; chill.

Spoon fool into individual dessert dishes and decorate with grated orange peel, additional fresh cranberries and fresh leaves, if desired.

Makes 4 servings.

VARIATION: Substitute 1/2 pound of plums for cranberries. Cook plums with 3 tablespoons of water and omit orange juice.

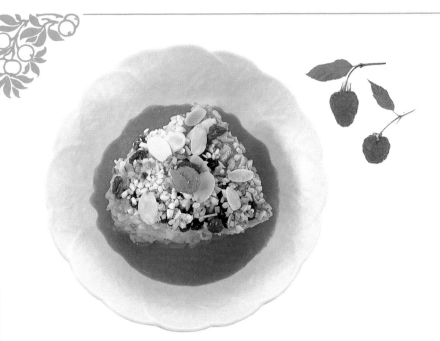

Cabinet Pudding

1/3 cup raisins
2 tablespoons rum, brandy or water
10 ounces chocolate or plain sponge cake
1/2 cup superfine sugar
1 cup chopped mixed nuts
4 eggs
2 cups milk
1/4 cup sliced almonds
1 recipe Raspberry Sauce, page 91, to serve
Fresh raspberries to decorate, if desired

Soak raisins in rum, brandy or water at least 1 hour. Preheat oven to 350F (175C). Lightly butter an oval baking dish.

Break up sponge cake coarsely and place in buttered dish. Add raisins and soaking liquid, then sprinkle with about 1/4 of sugar and all chopped mixed nuts. In a bowl, beat eggs with remaining sugar and whisk in milk. Pour into dish. Sprinkle with almonds.

Place dish in a roasting pan and add boiling water to come halfway up sides. Bake 1 to 1-1/2 hours, until custard is lightly set. Meanwhile, prepare Raspberry Sauce as directed. Serve pudding hot with sauce. Decorate with fresh raspberries, if desired.

Makes 6 servings.

VARIATION: Ratafias can be used in place of sponge cake, if desired.

NOTE: Stale leftover sponge cake is ideal for this pudding.

Creamy Almond Blancmange

1/2 cup whole blanched almonds
4 egg yolks
1/2 cup superfine sugar
1-1/2 cups milk
1 (1/4-oz.) envelope unflavored gelatin
    (1 tablespoon)
3 tablespoons water
1 cup whipping cream
Toasted sliced almonds and fresh herbs to
    decorate, if desired

Toast whole blanched almonds under broiler, turning frequently to brown evenly. Cool and grind coarsely in a coffee grinder or a food processor fitted with the metal blade.

In a bowl, beat egg yolks and sugar until thick and mousse-like. In a saucepan, bring milk almost to boiling point. Beat milk into egg mixture. Return to saucepan and cook over low heat, stirring until mixture has thickened sufficiently to coat back of a spoon; do not boil. Remove from heat and cool. In a small bowl, sprinkle gelatin over water and let stand 2 to 3 minutes, until softened. Set bowl of gelatin in a saucepan of hot water and stir until dissolved. Stir gelatin into milk mixture.

In another bowl, whip cream lightly. When milk mixture is at setting point, stir in ground almonds and fold in whipped cream. Spoon into a serving dish or individual dessert dishes and chill until set. Decorate with toasted sliced almonds and fresh herbs, if desired.

Makes 6 servings.

NOTE: For best flavor, grind whole nuts rather than buying them already ground. Toasting nuts helps to bring out more flavor.

Rose Custard Creams

1-1/4 cups milk
1-1/4 cups whipping cream
2 eggs
2 egg yolks
2 tablespoons plus 2 teaspoons superfine sugar
2 tablespoons plus 2 teaspoons rosé water

Marinated Fruit:
1 tablespoon plus 1 teaspoon rose water
1 tablespoon plus 1 teaspoon rosé wine
2 tablespoons plus 2 teaspoons powdered sugar
Petals from 2 scented roses
1 cup strawberries, sliced
1 cup raspberries, thawed if frozen
1 starfruit, sliced

Preheat oven to 300F (150C). In a saucepan, bring milk and whipping cream almost to boiling point.

In a bowl, beat eggs and egg yolks. Pour milk mixture into eggs, stirring well. Add sugar and rose water and stir until well blended. Divide mixture among 8 individual soufflé dishes. Stand dishes in a roasting pan and half-fill pan with cold water. Bake in oven about 1 hour or until custard has set. Remove dishes from water and refrigerate until cold.

To prepare marinated fruit, mix rose water, wine, powdered sugar and rose petals in a bowl. Add fruit; stir until well mixed. Cover with plastic wrap and chill until ready to serve. Turn custards out onto individual plates and serve with marinated fruit. Makes 8 servings.

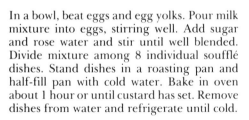

English Trifle

2 eggs
2 egg yolks
1 tablespoon plus 2 teaspoons superfine sugar
1-1/4 cups milk
1 teaspoon vanilla extract
2 tablespoons Madeira wine
1 tablespoon brandy
20 sponge fingers
2 tablespoons raspberry jam
1-1/2 cups raspberries, thawed if frozen
1-1/4 cups whipping cream
Angelica leaves to decorate
Vanilla cookies, if desired

To prepare custard, whisk whole eggs, egg yolks and sugar in a bowl until well blended. In a saucepan, bring milk and vanilla to boil. Pour over eggs in bowl, stirring thoroughly. Rinse out saucepan and strain custard through a sieve back into saucepan. Stirring continuously, cook over a gentle heat until thick but do not boil. Let stand until cold. In a small bowl, mix wine and brandy. Dip 1 sponge finger at a time into wine mixture. Spread with some jam and sandwich together with another dipped sponge finger. Place in bottom of a glass dish.

Repeat with remaining sponge fingers to cover bottom of dish. Pour remaining wine mixture over sponge fingers and cover with 2/3 of raspberries. In a bowl, whip cream until soft peaks form. Fold 2/3 of whipped cream into cold custard until well blended and smooth. Pour custard over raspberries in bowl. Place remaining whipped cream in a pastry bag fitted with a star nozzle. Pipe a border and decorate with angelica leaves and remaining raspberries. Serve with cookies, if desired. Chill until needed. Makes 8 servings.

Strawberry Yogurt Molds

2 cups strawberry-flavored yogurt
1 (1/4-oz.) envelope unflavored gelatin
   (1 tablespoon)
3 tablespoons water
1 pint strawberries

Pour yogurt into a bowl and chill.

In a small bowl, sprinkle gelatin over water and let stand 2 to 3 minutes, until softened. Set bowl of gelatin in a saucepan of hot water and stir until dissolved. Whisk into chilled yogurt, then pour into a wetted mold or 4 wetted individual molds. Chill until set.

To serve, slice strawberries. Turn out mold onto a serving plate and surround with sliced strawberries.

Makes 4 servings.

NOTE: For a softer texture, increase quantity of yogurt to 2-1/2 cups and set in a bowl rather than a mold.

Maple Bavarian Cream

1-1/2 tablespoons lemon juice
1-1/2 tablespoons water
1/2 (1/4-oz.) envelope unflavored gelatin
   (1-1/2 teaspoons)
1-1/4 cups whipping cream
1/4 cup plus 1 tablespoon maple syrup
1/3 cup crème fraîche
Additional maple syrup and langues de chat
   cookies to serve

In a small bowl, combine lemon juice and water. Sprinkle gelatin over lemon-water and let stand 2 to 3 minutes, until softened. In a bowl, whip cream lightly, adding 2-1/2 tablespoons of maple syrup.

Set bowl of gelatin in a saucepan of hot water and stir until dissolved. Stir in remaining maple syrup, then pour into whipped cream. Whisk again until cream stands in soft peaks.

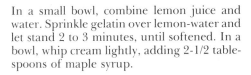

Fold crème fraîche into maple-cream mixture. Spoon into individual dessert dishes and chill until set. Spoon additional maple syrup over top and serve with cookies.

Makes 4 servings.

NOTE: Real maple syrup, as opposed to maple-flavored syrup, is very expensive and not always easy to obtain. It is worth seeking out for this dessert, as it greatly improves flavor.

Coeurs à la Créme

1 cup ricotta or cottage cheese
1 tablespoon plus 2 teaspoons superfine sugar
1 teaspoon lemon juice
1-1/4 cups whipping cream
2 egg whites
Fresh fruit or 1 recipe Raspberry Sauce, page
    91, and whipped cream, to serve, if desired

Line 4 heart-shaped molds with muslin. Press cheese through sieve into a bowl. Stir in sugar and lemon juice.

In a separate bowl, whip cream until stiff. Stir into cheese mixture. Whisk egg whites until stiff, then fold into the cheese mixture.

Spoon cheese mixture into the molds, place on a plate overnight to drain. To serve, unmold onto individual plates and gently remove the muslin. Serve hearts with fresh fruit or Raspberry Sauce and whipped cream, if desired.

Makes 4 to 6 servings.

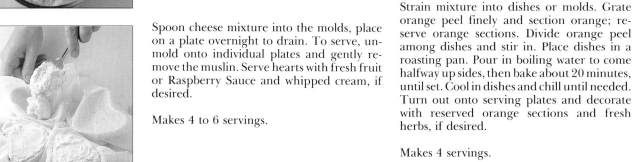

Orange Caramel Cream

1/2 cup granulated sugar
3 tablespoons water
3 eggs
2 tablespoons plus 2 teaspoons superfine sugar
1-1/4 cups milk
1 tablespoon orange flower water
1 orange
Fresh herbs to decorate, if desired

Preheat oven to 350F (175C). Warm 4 china ramekin dishes or 4 dariole molds. In a saucepan, combine granulated sugar and water and cook over low heat, stirring to dissolve sugar. Increase heat and boil steadily, without stirring, to a rich brown caramel.

Divide caramel among dishes or molds and tip to cover bottom and sides with caramel. Set aside. In a bowl, beat eggs and superfine sugar. In a saucepan, heat milk until almost boiling, then pour over egg mixture, beating constantly. Stir in orange flower water.

Strain mixture into dishes or molds. Grate orange peel finely and section orange; reserve orange sections. Divide orange peel among dishes and stir in. Place dishes in a roasting pan. Pour in boiling water to come halfway up sides, then bake about 20 minutes, until set. Cool in dishes and chill until needed. Turn out onto serving plates and decorate with reserved orange sections and fresh herbs, if desired.

Makes 4 servings.

NOTE: A dariole mold is a small cylindrical mold used for cooking pastries or vegetables.

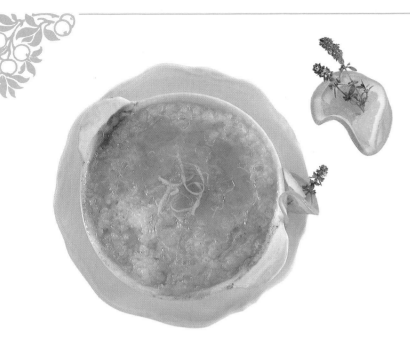

Caramel Rice

1/3 cup uncooked white short-grain rice
2-1/2 cups milk
1 vanilla bean
1/2 cup half and half
Juice of 1 orange
Superfine sugar
Shredded orange peel, orange slices and fresh
    herbs to garnish, if desired

In a saucepan, combine rice and milk and add vanilla bean. Simmer over very low heat 45 minutes to 1 hour, until rice is soft and creamy.

Remove vanilla bean and stir in half and half and orange juice. Spoon into a flameproof gratin or soufflé dish. Cool and chill until ready to serve.

Cover top of pudding thickly and evenly with sugar. Broil until sugar has caramelized. Garnish with shredded orange peel, orange slices and fresh herbs, if desired, and serve at once.

Makes 4 servings.

NOTE: If desired, chill pudding again before serving, but serve within 2 hours.

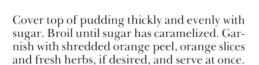

Queen of Puddings

2 cups milk
2/3 cup half and half
Grated peel of 1 small lemon
1-1/2 cups fresh white bread crumbs
3 tablespoons butter
1-1/4 cups superfine sugar
3 small eggs, separated
3 tablespoons raspberry jam
Orange slices, fresh raspberries and fresh
    herbs to garnish, if desired

Preheat oven to 350F (175C). Butter and oval flameproof dish. In a saucepan, combine milk, half and half and lemon peel.

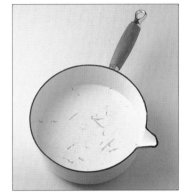

Heat milk mixture gently 5 minutes, then remove from heat and let stand 5 minutes to infuse. Place bread crumbs, butter and 1/4 of sugar in a bowl; pour warm milk on top. Stir until butter and sugar are dissolved. In a small bowl, beat egg yolks, then stir into bread crumb mixture. Pour into buttered dish and bake 45 to 50 minutes, until set. Remove from oven and cool slightly. Warm raspberry jam and spread over pudding.

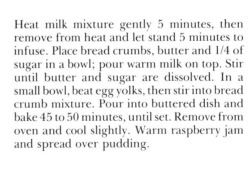

Reduce oven temperature to 325F (165C). In a large bowl, whisk egg whites until stiff, then fold in remaining sugar. Pile meringue on pudding and return to oven about 20 minutes, until meringue is crisp and golden. Serve warm or cold. Garnish with orange slices, fresh raspberries and herbs, if desired.

Makes 4 servings.

NOTE: Sieve raspberry jam to remove seeds, if desired.

Bread & Fruit Pudding

3/4 cup raisins and currants, mixed
8 thin slices white bread, buttered
2 tablespoons candied fruit, chopped
Superfine sugar

Custard:
1 egg yolk
1-1/4 cups milk
2/3 cup half and half
1 vanilla bean
1 teaspoon superfine sugar

In a bowl, cover raisins and currants with water; let stand to swell. Preheat oven to 350F (175C). Grease an oval baking dish.

Cut crusts from bread and sandwich 4 slices together. Cut in 4 squares and place in greased dish. Drain fruit and sprinkle fruit and chopped candied fruit over bread. Top with remaining bread, buttered side up.

To prepare custard, place egg yolk in a large glass measure. In a saucepan, combine milk, half and half, vanilla bean and sugar and bring almost to boiling point. Pour over egg, stir, then strain into dish, pouring down sides so top slices of bread are not soaked. Let stand 30 minutes. Sprinkle with sugar and place in a roasting pan. Pour in enough boiling water to come halfway up sides of dish and bake 45 to 50 minutes, until top is golden-brown. Serve immediately.

Makes 4 servings.

Charlotte Russe

16 ladyfingers
1 (1/4-oz.) envelope unflavored gelatin
   (1 tablespoon)
3 tablespoons water
4 egg yolks
1/3 cup superfine sugar
2-1/2 cups whipping cream
1 vanilla bean, split open
1-1/4 cups dairy sour cream
Additional whipped cream and 1-1/4 cups fresh
   raspberries to decorate

Line bottom of a 4-1/4-cup charlotte mold with waxed paper. Stand ladyfingers, pressing against each other, around sides of mold and trim to fit.

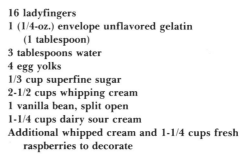

In a small bowl, sprinkle gelatin over water and let stand 2 to 3 minutes, until softened. In a bowl, whisk egg yolks and sugar until thick and mousse-like. In a saucepan, place 1-1/2 cups of whipping cream and vanilla bean and bring almost to a boil. Strain over egg mixture, stirring well. Pour back into saucepan and stir over low heat until mixture has thickened slightly; do not boil.

Strain into a clean bowl and add gelatin. Stir until dissolved. Cool, then set bowl in a larger bowl of iced water and stir until mixture thickens. Whip remaining cream with sour cream and fold into mixture. Pour into prepared mold, cover with plastic wrap and chill overnight. To serve, turn out onto a serving plate. Remove waxed paper and decorate with additional whipped cream and raspberries. Tie ribbon around pudding.

Makes 6 to 8 servings.

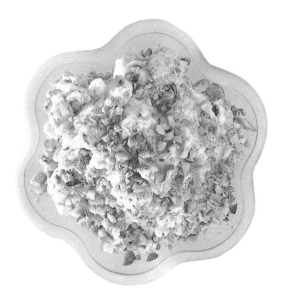

Atholl Brose

3 tablespoons regular rolled oats
1/3 cup whole blanched almonds
1-1/4 cups whipping cream
1/4 cup whiskey
1/4 cup orange flower honey
1 tablespoon lemon juice

Toast oats under broiler until brown. Toast almonds under broiler to brown evenly and chop finely.

In a large bowl, whip cream to soft peaks, then gradually whisk in whiskey, honey and lemon juice.

Fold oats and 1/2 of chopped almonds into creamy mixture and spoon into 4 dessert dishes. Chill. To serve, sprinkle remaining almonds on top of each pudding.

Makes 4 servings.

NOTE: This is a traditional Scottish dessert—delicious and very rich.

Cream & Sugar Parfaits

1-1/4 cups whipping cream
1 cup plain yogurt
1-1/2 cups packed light-brown sugar
Fresh strawberries or raspberries to serve, if
desired

In a large bowl, whip cream to stiff peaks. Fold in yogurt.

Half fill 4 glasses with creamy mixture. Sprinkle with about 1/3 of brown sugar. Spoon remaining creamy mixture into glasses, then pile on remaining brown sugar.

Refrigerate overnight. Serve puddings with fresh strawberries or raspberries, if desired.

Makes 4 servings.

NOTE: The brown sugar melts and forms a fudgy layer in these parfaits. They must be prepared a day in advance to allow for this.

Rice & Fruit Mold

1/2 cup plus 1 tablespoon uncooked white
    short-grain rice
3-3/4 cups milk
Superfine sugar to taste
Grated peel and juice of 1 orange
1 (1/4-oz.) envelope unflavored gelatin
    (1 tablespoon)
8 ounces mixed fresh fruit such as grapes,
    bananas and strawberries
2 tablespoons whipping cream
2 egg whites
1 recipe Raspberry Sauce, page 91, if desired

In a saucepan, combine rice and milk. Simmer 40 minutes to 1 hour, until creamy. Sweeten rice with sugar and stir in orange peel.

In a small bowl, sprinkle gelatin over orange juice and let stand 2 to 3 minutes, until softened. Set bowl of gelatin in a saucepan of hot water and stir until dissolved. Stir gelatin into rice; cool. Halve and seed grapes, finely slice bananas and cut strawberries in quarters. Reserve a few strawberries and grapes for decoration. Fold remaining fruit into rice. In a bowl, whip cream lightly.

In a separate bowl, whisk egg whites until stiff. Fold whipped cream, then egg whites into rice mixture. Turn rice into a glass serving bowl or a lightly oiled ring mold and refrigerate until set. Meanwhile, prepare Raspberry Sauce, if desired, as directed. To serve, turn dessert out of mold onto a serving plate and garnish with reserved fruit. Serve with sauce, if desired.

Makes 4 to 6 servings.

NOTE: Turn out molded puddings onto a wetted serving plate. The pudding will then slide easily over the plate and can be centered. Dry the plate around the pudding with paper towels.

Amaretti Cheese Whip

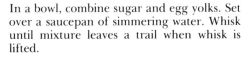

1/4 cup superfine sugar
2 eggs, separated
1-1/4 cups mascarpone cream cheese, beaten
Finely grated peel 1 tangerine
3/4 cup chopped mixed glacé fruits
1/4 cup broken Amaretti cookies (macaroons)
1 tablespoon plus 1 teaspoon Amaretto liqueur
2/3 cup whipping cream

Decoration:
Glacé fruits and Amaretti cookies (macaroons)
    to decorate

In a bowl, combine sugar and egg yolks. Set over a saucepan of simmering water. Whisk until mixture leaves a trail when whisk is lifted.

Stir in cream cheese, tangerine peel, chopped glacé fruits, broken Amaretti cookies and liqueur. In a small bowl, whisk egg whites until stiff. In another small bowl, whip whipping cream until thick. Add egg whites and whipped cream to cream cheese mixture and fold in carefully until mixture is evenly blended. Cover with plastic wrap and chill until needed.

Just before serving, divide mixture among 6 to 8 small dishes. Decorate with glacé fruit and Amaretti cookies. Makes 6 to 8 servings.

Festive Cheesecake

1-1/2 (8-oz.) pkgs. cream cheese
2/3 cup fromage frais
2 eggs, separated
1 tablespoon plus 1 teaspoon Grenadine syrup
1/3 cup Marsala wine
1 tablespoon plus 2 teaspoons plain gelatin
3 tablespoons water
1 starfruit, sliced
2 figs, sliced
10 kumquats, sliced
Melon balls
Seedless green and black grapes, halved
Holly sprigs and additional kumquat slices to
    decorate

Crust:
1/4 cup butter
1 tablespoon light corn syrup
2 cups vanilla wafer crumbs

To prepare crust, gently heat butter and syrup in a saucepan until melted. Stir in vanilla wafer crumbs and press into bottom of a 9-inch spring-form pan. To prepare filling, beat cream cheese, fromage frais, egg yolks, 1 tablespoon Grenadine syrup and 2 tablespoons wine in a bowl until smooth. In a small bowl, sprinkle gelatin over water and let stand until softened. Stand bowl in saucepan of hot water and stir until dissolved and quite hot. Stir gelatin into cheesecake mixture and let stand until thickened. In a bowl, whisk egg whites until stiff. Fold egg whites into cheesecake mixture until well blended and smooth. Pour over crust. Shake to level top and chill until set.

In a bowl, place all fruits. In a saucepan, heat remaining Grenadine syrup and wine until hot but not boiling. Pour over fruit and let stand until cold. Drain liquid into saucepan. Arrange fruit over top of cheesecake. Boil liquid until syrupy, brush fruit to glaze. Cut in slices to serve. Decorate with holly sprigs and additional kumquat slices. Makes 8 servings.

Austrian Cheesecake

4 tablespoons cup butter, softened
2/3 cup superfine sugar
1 cup plus 1 tablespoon cottage cheese, sieved
2 eggs, separated
1/2 cup ground almonds
1/3 cup fine semolina
Grated peel and juice of 1 small lemon
Powdered sugar
1 recipe Raspberry Sauce, page 91, or Hot
    Lemon Sauce, page 93
Lemon twists to garnish, if desired

Preheat oven to 375F (190C). Butter a deep 8-inch cake pan and dust with flour. In a large bowl, cream butter, sugar and cottage cheese until soft and fluffy.

Beat egg yolks into cheese mixture, then fold in ground almonds, semolina and lemon peel and juice. In a separate bowl, whisk egg whites until stiff and carefully fold into cottage cheese mixture.

Turn mixture into buttered pan and bake about 50 minutes, until golden-brown and springy to touch. Cool 20 minutes in pan, then turn out and dust with powdered sugar. Prepare Raspberry Sauce or Hot Lemon Sauce as directed. Serve cheesecake warm or cold with sauce. Garnish with lemon twists, if desired.

Makes 6 servings.

NOTE: If desired, place a paper doily on cheesecake, then dust with powdered sugar. Remove doily and serve.

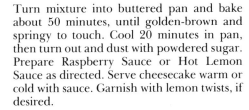

Oeufs à la Neige

4 eggs, separated
1/2 teaspoon cornstarch
1/3 cup superfine sugar
1/2 cup milk
1-1/4 cups half and half
1 vanilla bean
1 tablespoon orange flower water
1 tablespoon toasted whole almonds and orange peel strips to decorate, if desired

In a bowl, cream egg yolks, cornstarch and 1/2 of sugar. In a saucepan, scald milk, half and half and vanilla bean.

Pour hot milk over egg yolks, whisking constantly. Pour egg mixture back into pan; set over a pan of simmering water and cook gently, stirring constantly, until consistency of thick cream. Cool, remove vanilla bean and stir in orange flower water. In a large bowl, whisk egg whites until stiff, add remaining sugar and whisk again.

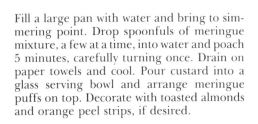

Fill a large pan with water and bring to simmering point. Drop spoonfuls of meringue mixture, a few at a time, into water and poach 5 minutes, carefully turning once. Drain on paper towels and cool. Pour custard into a glass serving bowl and arrange meringue puffs on top. Decorate with toasted almonds and orange peel strips, if desired.

Makes 4 servings.

Pink Grapefruit Cheesecake

8 ounces graham crackers
8 tablespoons butter, melted
2 pink grapefruits
1 (1/4-oz.) envelope unflavored gelatin (1 tablespoon)
1 (8-oz.) package cream cheese, softened
2/3 cup half and half
2 tablespoons superfine sugar
Grated peel and juice of 1 lemon
4 egg whites

Crush crackers to crumbs and mix with melted butter.

Press 2/3 of crumb mixture over bottom of a 9-inch loose-bottom or springform pan and chill. Cut off peel and pith from grapefruits, holding over a bowl to catch juice. Cut out sections from between membranes and set aside. Squeeze membranes into bowl to extract juice. Sprinkle gelatin over juice and let stand 2 to 3 minutes, until softened. Set bowl of gelatin in a pan of hot water and stir until dissolved. In a bowl, beat cream cheese, half and half and sugar. Stir in gelatin and lemon peel and juice.

In a large bowl, whisk egg whites until stiff. Fold into creamy mixture. Pour over crust and refrigerate until set. To serve, remove cheesecake from pan and decorate with reserved grapefruit sections. Press remaining crumbs evenly into sides of cheesecake.

Makes 6 to 8 servings.

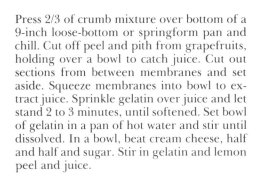

SOUFFLÉS, OMELETTES, MOUSSES & MERINGUES

Hot Chocolate Soufflé

2 tablespoons superfine sugar
4 ounces semisweet chocolate
2 tablespoons brandy or coffee
4 eggs, separated, plus 2 extra whites
1 recipe Dark Chocolate Sauce, page 92, or
    Bitter Mocha Sauce, page 93, if desired
    and powdered sugar to serve

Preheat oven to 400F (205C). Butter a 4-cup soufflé dish and dust with 1 tablespoon of superfine sugar. Break chocolate in pieces. In top of a double boiler or a bowl set over a pan of simmering water, place chocolate pieces and brandy or coffee.

Cook over medium heat, stirring until smooth. Remove from heat and beat in remaining superfine sugar and egg yolks. In a bowl, whisk egg whites until stiff but not dry. Fold 1 tablespoon into chocolate mixture. Scrape chocolate mixture into egg whites and, using a metal spoon, quickly fold together.

Pour into buttered soufflé dish and place on a baking sheet. Bake 15 to 18 minutes, until risen and just set. Meanwhile prepare Dark Chocolate Sauce or Bitter Mocha Sauce, if desired, according to directions. Dust soufflé with powdered sugar and serve immediately with sauce, if desired.

Makes 4 servings.

NOTE: Take care when melting chocolate not to overheat. It loses its gloss and becomes very thick, making it difficult to combine with other ingredients.

Red Berry Soufflé

2 tablespoons butter
1/2 cup plus 1 tablespoon superfine sugar
1-3/4 cups mixed red berries, thawed if frozen
1 tablespoon strawberry liqueur or crème de
    cassis
5 egg whites
Powdered sugar to serve

Preheat oven to 350F (175C). Butter a 4-cup soufflé dish, then dust with 1 tablespoon of superfine sugar.

In a blender or food processor, process remaining superfine sugar, berries and liqueur to a puree. Pour into a bowl. In a separate bowl, whisk egg whites until stiff but not dry. Fold 1 tablespoon of whipped egg whites into puree. Pour puree onto whipped egg whites and, using a metal spoon, carefully fold in.

Spoon mixture into prepared soufflé dish. Place dish on a baking sheet and bake 25 to 30 minutes, until risen and just set. Dust with powdered sugar and serve immediately.

Makes 6 servings.

NOTE: If desired, spoon mixture into 6 individual soufflé dishes and bake 15 to 20 minutes.

Coffee Chiffon Desserts

1/4 cup butter
3 tablespoons light corn syrup
2 cups vanilla wafer crumbs
2/3 cup whipping cream, whipped, and liqueur coffee beans to decorate

Filling:
3 tablespoons cornstarch
1/4 cup superfine sugar
1 tablespoon instant coffee granules
1-1/4 cups milk
2 eggs, separated
1 tablespoon plus 2 teaspoons plain gelatin
3 tablespoons hot water
1-1/4 cups whipping cream

In a saucepan, heat butter and corn syrup until melted. Stir in cookie crumbs and mix together evenly. Divide mixture among 8 plastic wrap-lined tiny molds and press mixture evenly over bottom and up sides of molds. Chill. To prepare filling, mix cornstarch, sugar, coffee and milk in a saucepan. Bring to a boil, stirring constantly, and cook 2 minutes. Remove from heat. Beat in egg yolks. In a small bowl, sprinkle gelatin over hot water; let stand to soften. Set bowl in a saucepan of hot water. Stir until dissolved and quite hot. Stir gelatin into coffee mixture and let stand until thick but not set.

In a small bowl, whisk egg whites until stiff. In a medium bowl, whip cream until thick. Fold egg whites and whipped cream evenly into coffee mixture. Divide mixture among molds, filling each to top. Cover and chill. To serve, invert molds onto serving plates; remove plastic wrap.

To decorate, place whipped cream in a pastry bag fitted with a star nozzle. Pipe around bottom of molds. Decorate with coffee beans. Makes 8 servings.

Soufflé Lime & Chocolate Layer

4 eggs, separated
1/3 cup superfine sugar
1 tablespoon plain gelatin
3 tablespoons water
Finely grated peel and juice 1 lime
2 (1-oz.) squares semi-sweet chocolate, melted
1-1/4 cups whipping cream
Chocolate curls and lime peel to decorate

In a bowl, combine egg yolks and sugar. Set over a saucepan of simmering water. Whisk until pale and thick. Remove bowl from pan. Continue to whisk until mixture leaves a trail when whisk is lifted. In a small bowl, sprinkle gelatin over water and let soften 2 to 3 minutes. Stand bowl in saucepan of hot water and stir until dissolved and quite hot.

Stir gelatin into egg yolk mixture until well blended. Pour 1/2 of mixture into another bowl. Stir grated lime peel and juice into 1 mixture and chocolate into remaining mixture until well blended. In a small bowl, whisk egg whites until stiff. In another small bowl, whip cream until thick. Add 1/2 of egg whites and cream to each mixture and fold in carefully until evenly blended.

Place alternate spoonfuls of each mixture into 8 small glasses. Let stand until set, then decorate with chocolate curls and lime twists. Makes 8 servings.

Omelet-Meringue Surprise

6 eggs
2 tablespoons sugar
2 almond macaroons, crushed
2 tablespoons half and half
1 tablespoon butter
5 tablespoons blackberry or black
　currant jam
1/4 cup finely chopped walnuts

Topping:
2 egg whites
1/2 cup sugar
2 tablespoons powdered sugar, sifted

Preheat oven to 425F (220C). In a medium-size bowl, beat eggs, sugar, macaroons and half and half until thick and creamy. Set 7-inch omelet pan over low heat to become thoroughly hot. Add half the butter and heat until sizzling but not brown. Pour in half the egg mixture. Cook until just set. Lift onto a warm heatproof plate. Repeat with remaining butter and egg mixture. Warm jam in a small saucepan over low heat. Stir in walnuts. Spread over first omelet; top with second omelet.

For topping: In a bowl, beat egg whites until stiff; gradually beat in sugar. Pipe meringue over omelets, *sealing completely* (do not leave even a pin-sized area unsealed or meringue will begin to shrink). Sprinkle with powdered sugar. Bake 3 minutes. Serve immediately. Serves 4.

Soufflé Omelet Surprise

2-1/2 cups vanilla ice cream
8 oz. raspberries or strawberries
2 tablespoons kirsch
2 tablespoons sugar
1 thin, 8- or 9-inch sponge cake
3 eggs, separated
Sugar

Before proceeding with recipe, line 8- or 9-inch cake pan (use same size as sponge cake) with plastic wrap; spoon in ice cream, spreading evenly. Freeze until very hard. Preheat oven to 425F (220C). Reserve a few raspberries or strawberries for decoration. Leave remaining raspberries whole or slice remaining strawberries if using instead. Combine berries with kirsch and 1 tablespoon sugar in a small bowl. Place sponge cake on flat heatproof plate. Spoon fruit and juice over cake.

In a medium-size bowl, beat egg yolks with remaining 1 tablespoon sugar until thick and creamy. In another bowl, beat egg whites until stiff. Fold into yolks. Remove ice cream by lifting edges of plastic wrap; peel off plastic. Set ice cream over berries. Quickly spread egg mixture over ice cream and cake, covering completely. Sprinkle with sugar. Bake 3 minutes. Decorate with reserved raspberries or strawberries and serve immediately. Serves 6.

Soufflé Omelette

3 eggs, separated
1 tablespoon half and half
2 teaspoons superfine sugar
1 tablespoon butter
2 tablespoons raspberry jam
Powdered sugar
Fresh raspberries and leaves to garnish, if
   desired

Preheat oven to 400F (205C). In a bowl, beat egg yolks, half and half and superfine sugar lightly. In a large bowl, whisk egg whites until stiff. Add egg yolk mixture to whisked egg whites and carefully fold together.

In an omelette pan, melt butter over medium heat and pour egg mixture into pan. Spread evenly and cook about 1 minute, until brown underneath. Bake in oven 5 minutes, until top is set. Meanwhile, heat 2 metal skewers either in a gas flame or under a broiler until they are red hot and glowing.

Summer Soufflé Omelet

6 oz. mixed fruits such as black currants,
   red currants, raspberries and
   strawberries
3 tablespoons crème de cassis or water
1 tablespoon sugar
1 tablespoon arrowroot

Basic Soufflé Omelet (see right)

1 tablespoon powdered sugar, sifted

Prepare filling before making omelet. Put fruit in a medium-size saucepan with crème de cassis and sugar. Cook over medium heat until juices run. Remove from heat. Mix arrowroot with a little water then stir into fruit. Return to heat and cook, stirring, until thickened. Let cool.

Prepare omelet and place on a warm heat-proof plate. Spoon cooled filling over half the omelet and fold over. Sprinkle with powdered sugar. Decorate with fruit and leaves, if desired. Serves 2.

Warm jam slightly. Remove omelette from oven and quickly spread with jam. Fold over and transfer to a serving plate. Sift powdered sugar thickly over omelette. Holding hot skewers with thick oven gloves, mark a criss-cross pattern in powdered sugar by pressing in skewers. Garnish with fresh raspberries and leaves, if desired, and serve immediately.

Makes 2 servings.

Amaretti & Almond Mousse

1/2 cup whole blanched almonds
2 ounces amaretti cookies (macaroons)
3 eggs plus 2 egg yolks
1/3 cup superfine sugar
1 (1/4-oz.) envelope unflavored gelatin
   (1 tablespoon)
2 tablespoons lemon juice
1 to 2 tablespoons amaretto or kirsch
1-1/4 cups whipping cream

Toast nuts under broiler until brown. In a food processor fitted with the metal blade, process nuts and cookies to crumbs.

In a bowl, whisk eggs, extra yolks and sugar until thick and mousse-like. In a small bowl, sprinkle gelatin over lemon juice and let stand 2 to 3 minutes, until softened. Set bowl of gelatin in a saucepan of hot water and stir until dissolved. Reserve 1/4 of crumbs. Add gelatin, amaretto or kirsch and remaining crumbs to egg mixture. Whip cream stiffly. Reserve 1/3 of whipped cream and fold remaining into egg mixture.

Pour creamy mixture into a 4-cup soufflé dish and chill until set. Just before serving, using a pastry bag fitted with a star nozzle, pipe rosettes of reserved whipping cream on mousses and sprinkle with reserved crumbs.

Makes 6 to 8 servings.

NOTE: Amaretto is a very sweet liqueur made from almonds. Using kirsch instead gives a subtler flavor and makes the dessert less sweet.

Mango Mousse

1 (16-oz.) can mangoes
Juice of 1/2 lemon
1 to 2 tablespoons superfine sugar
1 (1/4-oz.) envelope unflavored gelatin
   (1 tablespoon)
1/4 cup plus 1 tablespoon water
1-1/4 cups whipping cream
Fresh mango slices and lemon peel strips to
   decorate

Drain mangoes well. In a blender or food processor fitted with the metal blade, process mangoes and lemon juice to a puree. Sweeten to taste with sugar.

In a small bowl, sprinkle gelatin over water and let stand 2 to 3 minutes, until softened. Set bowl of gelatin in a saucepan of hot water and stir until dissolved. Stir gelatin into puree, then chill until almost set. In a bowl, whip cream lightly and gently fold into mango mixture.

Pour mixture into a glass serving bowl or individual serving dishes and refrigerate until set. Decorate with fresh mango slices and lemon peel strips to serve.

Makes 4 servings.

NOTE: When folding whipped cream and/or egg whites into gelatin mixture, the gelatin mixture must be almost set. If folded in too soon, the mixture will separate with the gelatin on bottom and froth on top.

Passion-Fruit Mousse

12 passion fruit
Juice and grated peel of 1 large orange
5 eggs
1/2 cup superfine sugar
1 (1/4-oz.) envelope unflavored gelatin
 (1 tablespoon)
3 tablespoons water
1-1/4 cups whipping cream
Additional passion fruit, if desired
Mint leaves to garnish, if desired

Cut passion fruit in half and scoop out pulp.
In a saucepan, combine pulp and orange
juice. Heat gently 2 to 3 minutes, then chill.

In a large bowl, whisk orange peel, eggs and
sugar until thick and mousse-like. In a small
bowl, sprinkle gelatin over water and let stand
2 to 3 minutes, until softened. Set bowl of
gelatin in a saucepan of hot water and stir
until dissolved. Add to egg mixture. Sieve
chilled passion-fruit mixture and stir 1/2 of
mixture into mousse. Chill remainder.

In a bowl, whip cream lightly and fold into
mousse mixture. Spoon into a soufflé dish or
glass serving bowl and chill. Serve with additional passion fruit, if desired, and garnish
with mint leaves, if desired. Serve reserved
passion-fruit mixture as a sauce.

Makes 6 servings.

NOTE: Place passion fruit in a bowl with un-
ripe fruits, and they will ripen quicker.

Minty Chocolate Mousse

6 ounces semisweet chocolate
1-1/4 cups whipping cream
1 egg
Pinch of salt
Few drops peppermint extract
1/2 recipe Chocolate Mousse Cups, page 64,
 if desired
Coarsely grated semisweet chocolate to
 decorate, if desired.

Sugared Mint Leaves:
Mint leaves
1 small egg white
Superfine sugar

Break up chocolate in small pieces and place
in a blender or food processor fitted with the
metal blade.

In a small saucepan, heat whipping cream
until almost boiling. Pour cream over chocolate and blend 1 minute. Add egg, salt and
peppermint extract and blend 1 minute
more. Pour into individual ramekin dishes or
chocolate cups, if desired, and refrigerate
overnight.

To prepare decoration, wash and dry mint
leaves. In a shallow bowl, lightly whisk egg
white and dip in mint leaves to cover. Dip
leaves into sugar, shake off any excess and let
stand on waxed paper until hardened. To
serve, decorate mousses with sugared mint
leaves and grated chocolate, if desired.

Makes 4 to 6 servings.

NOTE: Peppermint extract has a very strong
flavor; use it sparingly.

— Meringues with Honey & Almonds —

Meringues:
4 egg whites
1/2 cup superfine sugar

To Serve:
2 tablespoons honey
2 tablespoons toasted sliced almonds
1-1/4 cups whipping cream, if desired

Fresh herbs to decorate, if desired

Preheat oven to 300F (150C). Line 2 baking sheets with parchment paper. To prepare meringues, in a large bowl, whisk egg whites until stiff but not dry.

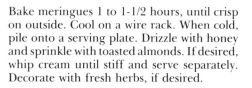

Sprinkle 1 tablespoon of sugar over egg whites and whisk 1 minute more. Sprinkle 1/2 of remaining sugar over egg whites and, using a metal spoon, fold in carefully. Then fold in remaining sugar. Using a pastry bag fitted with a plain or star nozzle, pipe 12 to 16 small circles or ovals onto prepared baking sheets, or drop 12 to 16 spoonfuls of meringue onto prepared baking sheets.

Bake meringues 1 to 1-1/2 hours, until crisp on outside. Cool on a wire rack. When cold, pile onto a serving plate. Drizzle with honey and sprinkle with toasted almonds. If desired, whip cream until stiff and serve separately. Decorate with fresh herbs, if desired.

Makes 12 to 16 meringues.

NOTE: An electric mixer can be used to make meringues. Separate eggs carefully; whites will not whip if there is any yolk in them.

— Chocolate-Dipped Meringues —

1 recipe Meringues (see left)
4 ounces semisweet chocolate
2 tablespoons water
1-1/4 cups whipping cream
Fresh strawberries, sliced, to garnish

Prepare 12 meringues as directed.

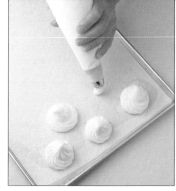

Break up chocolate. In top of a double boiler or bowl set over a pan of simmering water, melt chocolate pieces with water, stirring occasionally, until melted and smooth. Dip flat underside of meringues into melted chocolate to cover. Set on waxed paper on their sides for chocolate to harden.

Whip cream in a bowl. In a piping bag fitted with a star nozzle, pipe whipped cream onto 6 meringues. Sandwich in pairs with remaining 6 meringues. Place meringues in paper cups or on individual plates and garnish with sliced strawberries.

Makes 6 servings.

NOTE: A few drops of red food coloring can be added to meringue mixture to color it pink, if desired.

Ginger Marron Glacé

Pavlova:
3 egg whites
1 cup superfine sugar
1 teaspoon white vinegar
1 teaspoon orange flower water
1 teaspoon cornstarch
Mint sprigs to decorate

Filling:
1-1/4 cups whipping cream
3 pieces preserved stem ginger in syrup,
  chopped
10 whole marrons glacés, cut in pieces
Vanilla ice cream

Preheat oven to 275F (135C). Line 2 baking sheets with parchment paper. Mark 10 (3-inch) circles and invert paper.

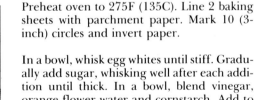

In a bowl, whisk egg whites until stiff. Gradually add sugar, whisking well after each addition until thick. In a bowl, blend vinegar, orange flower water and cornstarch. Add to meringue and whisk until very thick and glossy. Place meringue in a large pastry bag fitted with a small star nozzle. Pipe a shell edging around marked lines, then fill in center with a thin layer of meringue. Pipe a second shell edging on top of first edge. Bake 45 minutes. Turn off oven and leave meringues in to cool. Remove when cold. Store in an airtight container until needed.

In a bowl, whip cream until thick. Place 1/2 of whipped cream into pastry bag fitted with a nozzle. Fold chopped ginger into remaining whipped cream and spoon into center of each meringue. Just before serving, top each with balls of ice cream and a marron glacé. Decorate with mint sprigs. Makes 10 servings.

Festive Meringues

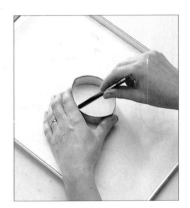

1-1/2 cups mixed glacé fruits, chopped
2 tablespoons plus 2 teaspoons Strega liqueur
1 cup whipping cream
1/4 cup plain yogurt
1 starfruit, thinly sliced, to decorate

Meringue:
2 egg whites
1/2 cup superfine sugar

Preheat oven to 250F (120C). Line 2 baking sheets with waxed paper. Draw 5 oval shapes on each using a 2-1/2-inch oval cutter. Invert paper.

In a bowl, whisk egg whites until stiff. Whisk in sugar a little at a time, whisking thoroughly until thick and soft peaks form. Place mixture in a large pastry bag fitted with a medium star nozzle. Pipe shells of meringue around each oval shape, then fill in centers, making sure there are no gaps. Bake in oven 1-1/2 to 2 hours or until meringues are dry, crisp and lift off paper. Cool and store in an airtight container until needed. In a bowl, mix glacé fruit and liqueur and cover.

In a bowl, whip cream and yogurt until thick. Add 2/3 of glacé fruit and all liqueur. Fold in until just mixed. Spoon mixture onto each meringue. Decorate with starfruit slices and remaining glacé fruit. Makes 10 servings.

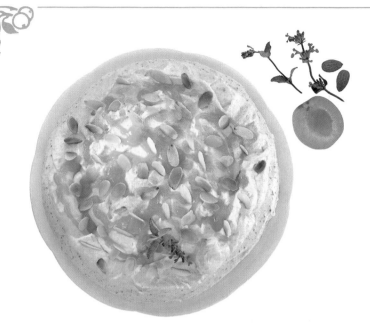

Dacquoise

1 cup whole blanched almonds
5 egg whites
1-1/2 cups superfine sugar
2-3/4 cups dried apricots
Juice of 1 lemon
Water
1-1/2 cups whipping cream
Toasted sliced almonds and fresh herbs to
    decorate, if desired

Toast whole almonds under a broiler, until evenly browned. Cool, then grind finely in a coffee grinder or a food processor fitted with the metal blade. Set aside. Preheat oven to 300F (150C). Line a baking sheet with parchment paper.

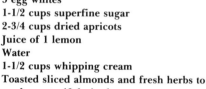

In a large bowl, whisk egg whites until stiff but not dry. Sprinkle with 2 tablespoons of sugar and whisk 1 minute. Using a metal spoon, fold in ground almonds and remaining sugar. Spoon meringue onto prepared baking sheet and spread evenly to a 10-inch circle. Bake 1-1/2 to 2 hours, until dry and light brown. Peel off paper and cool on a wire rack.

Place apricots and lemon juice in a saucepan. Cover with water and simmer over medium heat about 30 minutes, until tender; cool. In food processor, process apricots and a small amount of cooking liquid to make a thick puree. In a small bowl, whip cream stiffly and fold 1/2 of puree into whipped cream. Pile onto meringue and drizzle remaining puree over top. If necessary, thin puree with additional cooking liquid. Decorate with toasted almonds and fresh herbs, if desired.

Makes 6 to 8 servings.

Mini Pavlovas

2 egg whites
1-1/2 cups superfine sugar
1/2 teaspoon distilled white vinegar
1/2 teaspoon cornstarch
1/4 cup boiling water
1 recipe Tropical Flummery, page 9, or
    whipped cream and 1 recipe Black Currant
    & Cassis Sauce, page 90 to serve
Orange sections and fresh herbs to decorate, if
    desired

Preheat oven to 250F (120C). Line 2 baking sheets with parchment paper. In a large bowl, combine egg whites, sugar, vinegar and cornstarch; mix well.

Add boiling water and mix with an electric mixer until mixture is thick and white, about 10 minutes. Place 8 large spoonfuls on prepared baking sheets and spread in 4-inch circles. Using back of a spoon, make a slight depression in center of each.

Bake pavolvas about 30 minutes, until crisp on outside—they are like a marshmallow on inside. Remove from parchment paper and cool on wire racks. Prepare Tropical Flummery or Black Currant & Cassis Sauce as directed. To serve, fill centers with Tropical Flummery or with whipped cream with Black Currant & Cassis Sauce poured over top. Decorate with orange sections and fresh herbs, if desired.

Makes 8 servings.

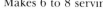

PANCAKES & WAFFLES

Basic Crepes

1 cup (4 oz.) all-purpose flour
Pinch of salt
2 eggs
1-1/4 cups milk
1 tablespoon butter, melted

Vegetable oil
Lemon juice and sugar *or* warmed jam

Sift flour and salt into a bowl. Make a well in the center and add the eggs and a little of the milk. Beat well with a wooden spoon, working in all the flour. Gradually beat in the remaining milk until bubbles form on top of batter. Stir in butter.

Add a small amount of oil to a 7-inch crepe pan—enough to barely cover the base—and place over high heat. Pour in 2 to 3 tablespoons batter and quickly tilt the pan so that the batter covers the base thinly and evenly. Cook for about 1 minute over high heat until lightly browned underneath.

Turn crepe with a metal spatula and cook other side for about 30 seconds. Keep crepe warm. Continue until batter is used. Serve with lemon juice and sugar, or with warmed jam. Makes 8 crepes.

Crepe Ribbons

1 recipe Basic Crepes (see left)
Vegetable oil for deep-frying

To Serve:
1 recipe Raspberry Sauce, page 91, Black Currant & Cassis Sauce, page 90 or Crème à la Vanille, page 91
Powdered sugar

Prepare pancakes according to directions; cool. Meanwhile, prepare Raspberry Sauce, Black Currant & Cassis Sauce or Crème à la Vanille according to directions.

Cut cold pancakes in ribbons or strips. Heat oil; test temperature by dropping in a small piece of pancake. It should sizzle furiously. Fry ribbons in batches, until crisp and golden. Remove with a slotted spoon and drain on crumpled paper towels. Keep warm.

Pile warm crepe ribbons onto a serving dish, dredge with powdered sugar and serve immediately with sauce.

Makes 4 servings.

NOTE: Pancakes can be prepared a day in advance, wrapped in foil and refrigerated or frozen. If frozen, thaw 1 to 2 hours at room temperature before cooking.

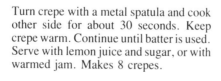

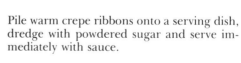

Honeyed Banana Topping

Basic Crepes (page 34)

3 medium-size bananas
2 teaspoons lemon juice
1/4 cup light honey
Pinch of nutmeg (preferably freshly grated)

Keep crepes warm while preparing topping. Peel bananas; slice in strips into a medium-size bowl. Add lemon juice and toss gently but thoroughly to coat banana.

Warm honey in a 1-quart saucepan over low heat. Add bananas and heat until just warm. Season with nutmeg. Spoon over crepes or pancakes. Serves 4.

Raspberry Sauce Topping

Basic Crepes (page 34)

1 (10- to 12-oz.) pkg. frozen raspberries in syrup, thawed
2/3 cup water
2 tablespoons sugar
1 tablespoon cornstarch
2 tablespoons cold water
Raspberry leaves to decorate

Keep crepes warm while preparing topping. Drain raspberry syrup into a small saucepan. Add 2/3 cup water and the sugar and bring to a boil over medium heat. Meanwhile, combine cornstarch with cold water in a small bowl; mix well. Stir in boiling liquid. Return to saucepan and bring to boil over low heat, stirring frequently, until sauce thickens.

Remove from heat and stir in raspberries. Heat gently, being careful not to break up fruit. Spoon over crepes or pancakes and decorate with raspberry leaves. Serves 4.

Banana Cream Topping

Basic Crepes (page 34)

2/3 cup whipping cream
2 large bananas
2 tablespoons powdered sugar
2 teaspoons lemon juice
1/2 teaspoon grated nutmeg
Pecan halves, if desired

Keep crepes warm while preparing topping. In a medium-size bowl, beat cream until soft peaks form. Peel bananas; mash them in another medium-size bowl with sugar and lemon juice. Fold the cream into the bananas. Season with nutmeg. To serve, fold crepes or pancakes into a cone shape and arrange on serving plates. Mound topping in center and garnish with pecans. Serves 4.

Orange Liqueur Topping

Basic Crepes (page 34)

1 medium-size orange
1/4 cup butter, softened
3/4 cup powdered sugar
2 tablespoons orange-flavored liqueur
Orange slices and slivered zest

Make crepes ahead and keep warm, or make crepes while topping chills. Grate zest (colored part only) from orange; transfer to a 1-cup glass measure. Squeeze orange juice and add to zest; set aside. In another small bowl, cream butter and sugar until light and fluffy.

Gradually add zest and orange juice to butter mixture and beat well. Gradually add orange liqueur and beat until soft and creamy. Chill for 30 minutes before serving. Pipe or spoon over crepes or pancakes and garnish with orange slices and slivered zest. Serves 4.

Fresh Lemon Topping

Basic Crepes (page 34)

2 lemons
1-1/4 cups water
1/4 cup sugar
2 tablespoons cornstarch
2 tablespoons lemon curd (purchased or homemade)

Keep crepes warm while preparing topping. Grate zest (colored part only) from lemons; transfer to small saucepan. Squeeze juice from lemons and add to pan. Reserve 3 tablespoons water; add remaining water and sugar to pan. Place over low heat and cook, stirring occasionally, until sugar is melted.

In a small bowl, combine reserved water with cornstarch. Stir in a small amount of the hot liquid and mix well. Return to pan and add lemon curd. Stir over low heat until sauce is thick and clear. Serve over crepes or pancakes. Garnish with thin strips of lemon zest, if desired. Serves 4.

Jamaican Banana Topping

Basic Crepes (page 34)

1/2 cup butter
3/4 cup packed brown sugar
1 lemon
3 medium-size bananas
2 tablespoons dark rum
Lemon twists and thin strips of lemon zest, if desired

Keep crepes warm while preparing topping. Combine butter and sugar in a small saucepan. Place over low heat and stir until butter is melted. Grate zest (colored part only) from lemon; squeeze juice from lemon. Stir zest and juice into saucepan and simmer, stirring, 1 minute.

Peel bananas; slice thinly. Stir into saucepan and cook gently 2 minutes. Remove from heat and stir in rum. Serve over crepes or pancakes. Garnish with lemon twists and lemon zest. Serves 4.

Apple Pancakes

1 cup all-purpose flour
Pinch of salt
1/2 cup milk
1/2 cup water
2 eggs
1 tablespoon vegetable oil
3 eating apples
2 teaspoons lemon juice
1 tablespoon brandy
2 teaspoons superfine sugar
Sliced apple and mint leaves to garnish, if
    desired

Sift flour and salt together. Combine milk and water. In a food processor fitted with the metal blade, process flour and salt, 1/2 of milk and water and eggs. Blend well, then add remaining milk and water and oil and blend again. Let stand 30 minutes. Process again before using.

Peel and core apples and slice very finely onto a plate. Sprinkle with lemon juice and brandy. Heat a 6- or 7-inch heavy-bottom skillet and grease lightly. Pour in 1 tablespoon of batter and roll pan to spread evenly. Place a few apple slices over pancake, then spoon a little more batter over apples. Cook 2 to 3 minutes, until batter is almost set. Place pan under a broiler to finish cooking batter.

Turn pancake out onto a plate and sprinkle with sugar. Prepare remaining pancakes. Garnish with sliced apple and mint leaves, if desired. Serve immediately.

Makes 4 servings.

VARIATION: Beer or cider can be used instead of milk.

NOTE: Mixing milk and water helps to lighten pancake batter.

Caribbean Crepes

7-inch crepes (page 34)

4 medium-size bananas
2 teaspoons lemon juice
2/3 cup whipping cream
2 tablespoons brown sugar
Grated nutmeg

Keep crepes warm while preparing filling. Peel bananas. Thinly slice one banana; sprinkle with lemon juice and set aside. In a medium-size bowl, whip cream until stiff; set aside about 1/4 for decoration.

Mash remaining bananas in a medium-size bowl. Fold into 3/4 whipped cream along with sugar and 1/2 teaspoon nutmeg. To serve, cut each crepe in half and fold into a cone shape. Fill with whipped cream mixture. Decorate with rosettes of reserved whipped cream and banana slices; sprinkle banana slices with additional nutmeg. Serves 4.

French Chestnut Crepes

7-inch crepes (page 34)

1 (8-oz.) can sweetened chestnut puree
6 tablespoons orange juice
1 tablespoon lemon juice
1 tablespoon rum
2 tablespoons butter, melted
1 tablespoon powdered sugar

Preheat oven to 300F (150C). Spread each crepe with chestnut puree. Fold into quarters and arrange in shallow heatproof dish. In a small bowl, combine orange juice, lemon juice and rum. Pour over crepes. Cover loosely with foil. Bake 30 minutes. Remove from oven and discard foil.

Preheat broiler. Brush crepes with butter and sprinkle with powdered sugar. Broil until glazed, about 2 minutes. Serve immediately. Serves 4.

Crepes Suzette

7-inch crepes (page 34)

1/3 cup unsalted butter
1/2 cup powdered sugar
3 tablespoons orange juice
1 tablespoon lemon juice
2 tablespoons orange-flavored liqueur

1 tablespoon brandy
Orange slices and bay leaves

Fold each crepe in quarters. Combine butter, sugar, orange juice and lemon juice in a large skillet. Heat gently until mixture is syrupy. Stir in liqueur.

Add crepes and turn each once to coat with sauce. Pour on brandy and light quickly with a match. Arrange on plates and garnish with orange slices and bay leaves. Serve immediately. Serves 4.

Mincemeat Crepe Gâteau

1 recipe Basic Crepes, page 34
1 (12-oz.) jar prepared mincemeat
1 eating apple
1 tablespoon brandy
Grated peel of 1 orange
Juice of 1/2 lemon
1 cup sliced almonds
1/4 cup apricot jam, sieved
Orange slices and fresh herbs to garnish, if
  desired

Prepare pancakes as directed. Preheat oven
to 350F (175C). Grease an 8-inch round baking dish. Spoon mincemeat into a saucepan.
Peel, core and chop apple and add to mincemeat.

Heat through, stirring occasionally, until
apple is tender. Remove from heat and stir in
brandy, orange peel, lemon juice and 3/4 of
almonds. Place 1 pancake in greased dish and
spread with a small amount of mincemeat
mixture. Layer gâteau, alternating pancakes
and mincemeat, ending with a pancake.

In a small saucepan, warm apricot jam and
pour over gâteau. Sprinkle with remaining
almonds and bake 15 minutes. Cut in wedges
and garnish with orange slices and fresh
herbs, if desired. Serve at once.

Makes 6 servings.

Cherry & Almond Layered Crepes

7-inch crepes (page 34)

1 (14-oz.) can cherries
6 tablespoons cherry jam
1 tablespoon lemon juice
1/2 cup ground almonds
2 eating pears, peeled and thinly sliced
1 tablespoon powdered sugar, sifted

Keep crepes warm while preparing filling. Drain cherries, reserving juice.
Measure jam into a medium-size saucepan. Place over low heat and warm just
until syrupy. Stir in 2 tablespoons reserved cherry juice, the lemon juice,
almonds and pears. Remove from heat
and stir in cherries.

Preheat oven to 325F (165C). Place one
crepe on a large heatproof plate. Spread
with some of the filling. Top with a
second crepe. Repeat until all the crepes
are used. Bake 10 minutes. Sprinkle with
powdered sugar. Cut into wedges and
serve immediately. Serves 4.

Lemon Meringue Layered Crepes

7-inch crepes (page 34)

Fresh Lemon Topping (page 36)

2 egg whites
1/4 cup sugar
2 oz. (1/2 cup) slivered almonds, toasted
Candied angelica

Keep crepes warm while preparing Fresh Lemon Topping. Place one crepe on a heatproof plate. Spread with some of topping. Cover with a second crepe. Repeat until all the crepes are used, finishing with a crepe on top.

Preheat oven to 425F (220C). In a medium-size bowl, beat egg whites until stiff; gradually beat in sugar. Cover top and sides of crepes with this meringue. Top with almonds. Bake until pale golden, about 2 minutes. Decorate with angelica. Cut in wedges and serve immediately. Serves 4.

Blackberry & Apple Stack

7-inch crepes (page 34)

1 lb. cooking apples
12 oz. blackberries
1/2 cup sugar
2 egg whites

Keep crepes warm while preparing filling. Peel and core apples; chop coarsely. In a medium-size saucepan, combine apples, blackberries and 1/4 cup sugar. Place over low heat and simmer until fruit is soft. Let stand 10 minutes to cool. Place one crepe on a heatproof plate. Spread with some of filling. Top with a second crepe. Repeat until all the crepes are used, finishing with a crepe on top.

Preheat oven to 325F (165C). In a medium-size bowl, beat egg whites until stiff; gradually beat in remaining sugar. Cover top and sides of crepes with this meringue. Bake until golden brown, about 15 minutes. Cut in wedges and serve immediately. Serves 4.

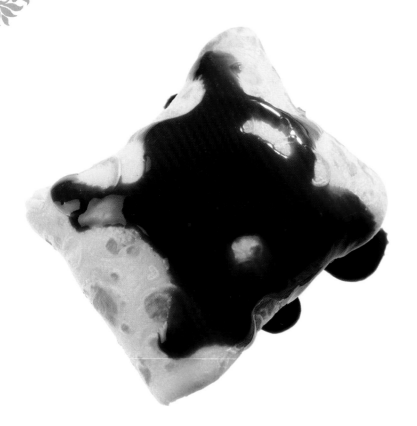

— Ice Cream Crepes & Chocolate Sauce —

Chocolate Sauce:
2/3 cup water
1/2 cup sugar
1/2 cup unsweetened cocoa powder

7-inch crepes (page 34)

1 pint vanilla ice cream
2 tablespoons cherry brandy

For sauce: Combine water and sugar in a small saucepan. Place over low heat and stir until sugar is dissolved. Bring to a boil, then simmer 1 minute. Add cocoa and return to boil, whisking constantly until sauce is smooth. Keep warm.

Cut ice cream into 8 cubes; wrap each one in a crepe. Arrange two crepes on each plate. Sprinkle with cherry brandy. Top with Chocolate Sauce and serve immediately. Serves 4.

— Cornmeal Pancakes —

1/2 cup (2 oz.) cornmeal
1-1/4 cups boiling water
1-1/4 cups milk
2 cups (8 oz.) all-purpose flour
2 tablespoons sugar
2 teaspoons baking powder
1 teaspoon salt
1 egg, beaten
2 tablespoons butter, melted

Vegetable oil
Butter and maple syrup

Pour the cornmeal into a small saucepan. Add water and simmer, stirring constantly, 5 minutes. Transfer to a medium-size bowl and beat in the milk. In another bowl, stir together flour, sugar, baking powder and salt. Beat into the cornmeal mixture. Beat in the egg and butter.

Place a heavy frying pan over high heat and grease lightly with oil. Pour in batter to make 3-inch rounds. Cook until surface is just set and covered with bubbles. Turn and cook other side until golden. Serve warm with butter and maple syrup. Makes 24 pancakes.

Basic Waffles

1-1/2 cups all-purpose flour
2 teaspoons baking powder
1/2 teaspoon salt
2 teaspoons sugar
2 eggs, separated
1 cup milk
1/3 cup butter, melted
Butter and maple syrup *or* bacon

Sift flour, baking powder and salt into a medium-size bowl. Stir in sugar. In another bowl, combine egg yolks, milk and butter and beat well. Add to dry ingredients and beat thoroughly. In another bowl, beat egg whites until stiff. Fold into batter.

Heat waffle iron, but do not grease. To test for correct heat, put 1 teaspoon water inside waffle iron, close and heat. When steaming stops, heat is correct for cooking waffles. Spoon 1 tablespoon batter into center of each compartment. Close and cook until puffed and golden brown. Lift out waffles with a fork. Serve hot with butter and maple syrup, or with bacon. Alternatively, serve waffles sandwiched together with whipped cream and decorated with fruit and powdered sugar. Makes 6 waffles.

Banana Nut Waffles

1-1/2 cups all-purpose flour
2 teaspoons baking powder
1/2 teaspoon salt
2 teaspoons sugar
2 eggs, separated
1 cup milk
1/3 cup butter, melted
3/4 cup finely chopped walnuts
2 medium-size bananas
2 tablespoons powdered sugar
1 tablespoon lemon juice

Sift flour, baking powder and salt into a medium-size bowl. Stir in sugar. In another bowl, combine egg yolks, milk and butter and beat well. Add to dry ingredients and beat thoroughly. Stir in 1 tablespoon of the walnuts. In another bowl, beat egg whites until stiff. Fold into batter.

Heat waffle iron, but do not grease. To test for correct heat, put 1 teaspoon water inside waffle iron, close and heat. When steaming stops, heat is correct for cooking waffles. Spoon 1 tablespoon batter into center of each compartment. Close and cook until puffed and golden brown. While waffles are cooking, peel bananas; slice into a bowl and sprinkle with sugar and lemon juice. Lift out waffles with a fork. Serve hot, topped with banana slices and sprinkled with remaining nuts. Makes 6 waffles.

Strawberry-Rum Waffles

6 Basic Waffles (page 43)

8 oz. fresh strawberries, thickly sliced
1/4 cup sugar
2 tablespoons light rum
6 scoops strawberry ice cream

While waffles are cooking, prepare topping. In a small bowl, combine strawberries, sugar and rum. Stir well and set aside until waffles are ready.

Spoon strawberries and liquid over hot waffles. Top each one with a scoop of ice cream. Serves 6.

Chocolate Cream Waffles

2/3 cup whipping cream
1-1/2 cups all-purpose flour
2 teaspoons baking powder
1/2 teaspoon salt
2 tablespoons sugar
2 eggs, separated
1 cup milk
1/3 cup butter, melted
2 oz. (2 squares) sweet dark chocolate, melted and cooled
1/2 teaspoon vanilla
Whipped cream and grated chocolate to decorate

In a small bowl, beat cream until soft peaks form. Spoon into serving bowl and refrigerate. Sift flour, baking powder and salt into a medium-size bowl. Stir in sugar. In another bowl, combine egg yolks, milk, butter, chocolate and vanilla and beat well. Add to dry ingredients and beat thoroughly. In another bowl, beat egg whites until stiff. Fold into batter.

Heat waffle iron, but do not grease. To test for correct heat, put 1 teaspoon water inside waffle iron, close and heat. When steaming stops, heat is correct for cooking waffles. Spoon 1 tablespoon batter into center of each compartment. Close and cook until puffed and crisp. Lift out waffles with a fork. Decorate with whipped cream and grated chocolate. Makes 6 waffles.

FRUIT DESSERTS

Fruit Fritters

4 baking or crisp tart eating apples
2 to 3 tablespoons calvados or cognac
3 tablespoons superfine sugar
1 cup all-purpose flour
Pinch of salt
2 eggs, separated
2/3 cup milk
1 tablespoon vegetable oil
Vegetable oil for deep-frying
Powdered sugar
Edible flowers to garnish, if desired

Peel, core and cut apples in rings.

In a shallow dish, mix calvados or cognac with 1/2 of sugar. Add apples, turning to coat. Let stand 30 minutes. Sift flour and salt into a large bowl and mix in remaining sugar. Make a well in center and drop in egg yolks. Using a wooden spoon, draw flour into yolks while gradually adding milk. Beat to a smooth batter, then let stand 30 minutes. In a separate bowl, whisk egg whites until stiff and fold into batter with 1 tablespoon oil.

Heat oil for deep frying to 385F (195C). Drain fruit and dip each ring into batter to coat. Deep-fry a few at a time, turning once, until puffed up and golden-brown. Drain on paper towels. Sprinkle with powdered sugar. Garnish with edible flowers, if desired. Serve hot.

Makes 4 servings.

VARIATION: Use pineapple, pears or bananas in place of apples, soaking fruit in an appropriate liqueur 30 minutes.

Caramel Fruit Kabobs

Selection of fruit such as 2 bananas, 2 pears, 1 small pineapple, 2 peaches, grapes and strawberries
1 recipe Mousseline Sauce, page 90, if desired
4 tablespoons butter, melted
2 tablespoons superfine sugar
Edible flowers and fresh herbs to garnish, if desired

Marinade:
1 tablespoon lemon juice
3 tablespoons brandy
1 to 2 tablespoons honey
1/2 cup orange juice
1 (3-inch) cinnamon stick, broken in pieces

In a large bowl, combine all marinade ingredients.

Cut bananas in 1-inch pieces. Peel and core pears and cut in chunks. Cut pineapple in thick slices; peel and discard core and cut pulp in chunks. Peel and pit peaches and cut pulp in chunks. Leave grapes whole. Add prepared fruit to marinade and stir very gently to coat evenly. Let stand 2 hours. Add whole strawberries to marinade 15 minutes before end of marinating time. Meanwhile, prepare Mousseline Sauce, if desired, as directed; keep warm.

Drain fruit, reserving marinade. Thread fruit onto 6 skewers. Brush with some of melted butter and sprinkle with some of sugar. Broil 7 to 8 minutes, turning frequently. Brush with remaining butter and sprinkle with remaining sugar while turning. Strain marinade into a saucepan and heat gently. Garnish kabobs with edible flowers and fresh herbs, if desired, and serve with marinade and sauce, if desired.

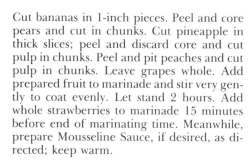

Makes 6 servings.

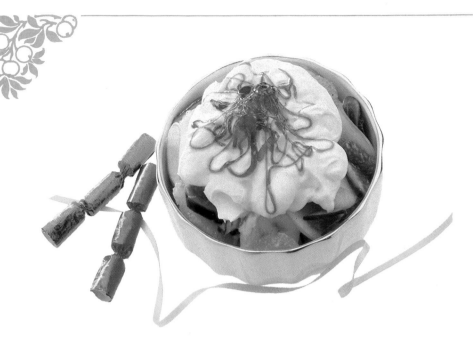

Frostie Fruit Brûlées

2 oranges
2 eating apples
2 figs
2 bananas
1 cup seedless grapes, halved
2 tablespoons Marsala wine
2-1/2 cups whipping cream
3/4 cup superfine sugar
1/4 cup boiling water

Using a sharp knife, cut orange peel away from flesh including white pith. Cut in between membrane to remove segments; place in a bowl. Cut apples into quarters; remove cores and slice thinly. Cut figs in thin wedges and slice bananas.

Gently combine all fruit and wine in bowl. Divide fruit among 6 individual dishes. In a bowl, whip cream until very thick. Spoon whipped cream evenly over fruit. Chill until ready to serve.

In a saucepan, heat sugar and water, stirring occasionally, until sugar has dissolved. Boil rapidly until syrup turns a golden brown color. Allow bubbles to subside, then drizzle caramel over top of fruit brûlées. Serve immediately. Makes 6 servings.

Lemon Belvoir Pudding

8 tablespoons butter, softened
1/2 cup superfine sugar
2 large egg yolks
2-1/2 cups fresh bread crumbs
Grated peel and juice of 2 lemons
1 teaspoon baking powder
1 recipe Hot Lemon Sauce, page 93
Powdered sugar
Lemon peel strips and fresh herbs to garnish,
    if desired

Generously butter a 4-cup charlotte mold. In a large bowl, cream butter and sugar until light and fluffy.

Beat in egg yolks and bread crumbs. When well mixed, stir in lemon peel and juice and baking powder. Spoon into buttered mold and cover top with a piece of foil pleated in middle. Tie securely around mold, then set mold in a saucepan of enough gently boiling water to come halfway up sides.

Steam 45 minutes to 1 hour. Check water in pan occasionally and add more boiling water as necessary. Meanwhile, prepare Hot Lemon Sauce as directed. Turn out pudding and dust with powdered sugar. Garnish with lemon peel strips and fresh herbs, if desired, and serve pudding hot with sauce.

Makes 4 servings.

NOTE: A charlotte mold is a plain cylindrical mold.

Apple Charlotte

1-1/2 pounds tart eating apples
1/2 cup packed light-brown sugar
8 tablespoons butter
Grated peel of 1 lemon
2-1/2 cups coarse fresh bread crumbs
Apple slices and fresh mint to decorate, if
    desired

Peel, core and slice apples. In a saucepan, place sliced apples, 1/3 cup of brown sugar, 2 tablespoons of butter and grated lemon peel. Simmer, covered, over low heat until soft. Beat until pureed.

In a skillet, melt remaining butter and sauté bread crumbs until golden-brown, stirring constantly to prevent burning. Stir in remaining brown sugar and cool.

Spoon 1/2 of apple mixture into 4 serving dishes and cover with 1/2 of crumb mixture. Top with remaining apples and crumbs and chill 2 hours before serving. Decorate with apple slices and fresh mint, if desired.

Makes 4 servings.

NOTE: To prevent brown sugar from hardening when stored, place a slice of apple in the container with it, and the brown sugar will stay soft.

Baked Stuffed Apples

3 tablespoons dark raisins
3 tablespoons golden raisins
1/4 cup plus 1 tablespoon ginger wine, Madeira
    or sweet sherry
4 large baking apples
3/4 cup toasted sliced almonds
1 to 2 tablespoons orange marmalade
Chilled whipped cream to serve

Preheat oven to 350F (175C). In a small bowl, combine raisins and ginger wine, Madeira or sweet sherry. Let stand several hours.

Wash and dry apples; do not peel. Core apples and score a line around middle of each apple. Place in an ovenproof dish. Drain raisins, reserving liquid. In a bowl, mix raisins, almonds and marmalade and fill apple cavities with fruit and nut mixture, pushing mixture down firmly. Pour strained liquid over apples.

Bake apples 45 minutes to 1 hour, until soft. Spoon a dollop of whipped cream on top of each apple and serve immediately.

Makes 4 servings.

Steamed Raisin Pudding

1 cup self-rising flour
3 tablespoons cornstarch
1 teaspoon baking powder
1/2 cup superfine sugar
8 tablespoons butter, softened
Grated peel and juice of 1 orange
2 eggs
3/4 cup golden raisins
1/3 cup chopped mixed candied citrus peel
Milk, if needed
1 recipe Mousseline Sauce, page 90, or Black
    Currant & Cassis Sauce, page 90.

Butter a 3-3/4-cup bowl or an 8-inch ring mold. Sift flour, cornstarch and baking powder onto a plate.

In a large bowl, cream sugar, butter and grated orange peel until light and fluffy. In a separate bowl, beat eggs with orange juice; beat gradually into butter mixture with 1 tablespoon of flour mixture. Fold in remaining flour with raisins and candied peel. Mixture should be a soft dropping consistency; if too stiff, add a small amount of milk.

Spoon mixture into prepared bowl or mold and cover with a piece of buttered foil pleated in middle. Tie securely around rim of bowl or mold and set in a saucepan of gently boiling water to come halfway up sides. Steam 1-1/2 to 2 hours. Meanwhile, prepare Mousseline Sauce or Black Currant & Cassis Sauce as directed. Turn out pudding and serve warm with sauce.

Makes 6 servings.

Cherry Clafouti

1-1/2 pounds pitted dark sweet cherries, thawed
    and drained if frozen
3/4 cup all-purpose flour
Pinch of salt
3 eggs
1/3 cup superfine sugar
2 cups milk
1 tablespoon cherry brandy or kirsch
Powdered sugar

Preheat oven to 400F (205C). Butter an oval baking dish and place cherries in it.

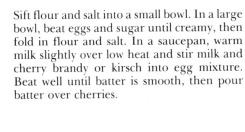

Sift flour and salt into a small bowl. In a large bowl, beat eggs and sugar until creamy, then fold in flour and salt. In a saucepan, warm milk slightly over low heat and stir milk and cherry brandy or kirsch into egg mixture. Beat well until batter is smooth, then pour batter over cherries.

Bake 30 minutes, until set and golden. Serve warm dusted with powdered sugar.

Makes 6 servings.

NOTE: Fresh cherries can taste a little bland when cooked. Add 1 to 2 drops almond extract to improve the flavor, if desired.

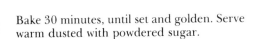

Round Christmas Pudding

3 cups mixed dried fruit
1/2 cup chopped prunes
1/3 cup chopped glacé cherries
1/2 cup chopped almonds
1/4 cup grated carrot
1/4 cup grated cooking apple
Finely grated peel and juice 1 orange
1 tablespoon molasses
1 tablespoon brandy
1/3 cup stout
1 egg, beaten
1/4 cup butter, melted
1/3 cup dark-brown sugar
3/4 teaspoon ground allspice
1/2 cup all-purpose flour
1 cup soft white bread crumbs
Holly sprigs to decorate
Additional brandy
1 recipe Brandy Butter (see page 95)

Combine mixed fruit, prunes, cherries, almonds, carrot, apple, orange peel and juice, molasses, brandy and stout. Stir in egg, butter, brown sugar, allspice, flour and bread crumbs. Cover with plastic wrap and refrigerate.

Using a 5-inch buttered spherical mold or a rice steamer mold lined with a double thickness of foil, fill each half of mold with mixture. Place 2 halves together, securing mold tightly.

Half-fill a saucepan with water. Bring to a boil and place mold in so water comes just below seam of mold. Cover and simmer 6 hours. Cool in mold, then turn out. When cold, wrap in foil. To reheat, unwrap and replace in mold. Cook as before in simmering water 2 to 3 hours. Decorate with holly. Warm brandy, spoon over pudding and light. Serve with Brandy Butter. Makes 8 servings.

Tipsy Fruit Jelly

3 lemons
1-1/4 cups water
1/2 cup superfine sugar
2/3 cup claret
2 tablespoons plain gelatin
1/4 cup hot water
12 oz. mixed fresh fruit such as grapes,
    lychees, pineapple, clementines, cut up
Additional fresh fruit and whipped cream to
    decorate

Using a vegetable peeler or sharp knife, pare peel from lemons. Squeeze juice. In a saucepan, combine peel and water and bring to a boil. Add sugar; stir until dissolved. Let stand until cold, then strain. Stir in lemon juice. Pour 1/3 of lemon mixture into a bowl. Add claret, stir until blended.

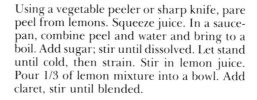

In a small bowl, sprinkle gelatin over hot water. Let stand until softened. Place bowl in a saucepan of hot water. Stir until dissolved and quite hot. Add 1/2 of gelatin to claret mixture, stirring well, and the remainder to lemon mixture, stirring well. Halve grapes and lychees, remove seeds and pits. Peel and slice pineapple and clementines.

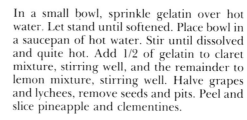

Arrange 1/4 of mixed fruit in bottom of 6 individual molds. Spoon enough lemon jelly over fruit to cover. Refrigerate until set. Arrange a second layer of fruit over set jelly layer and cover with claret jelly; refrigerate until set. Repeat to make another lemon fruit layer and claret fruit layer. Refrigerate until firmly set. Remove from molds by dipping into hand-hot water and invert onto a plate. Decorate with fresh fruit and piped whipped cream. Makes 6 servings.

Kissel

1-1/2 (16-oz.) cans black currants
1/2 (16-oz.) can pitted dark sweet cherries
1 tablespoon arrowroot
Grated peel and juice of 1 orange
1-3/4 cups fresh raspberries
2 tablespoons crème de cassis
Mint leaves to garnish, if desired

Drain black currants and cherries, reserving 2 cups juice. In a saucepan, bring juice to boil.

In a small bowl, mix arrowroot and orange juice and add to juices in pan. Stir in orange peel. Stir over medium heat until juice is thick and clear; syrup should boil 1 to 2 minutes to cook arrowroot.

Place black currants, cherries and raspberries in individual glass serving dishes. Pour thickened juice over fruit and cool. Stir in crème de cassis. Refrigerate until ready to serve. Garnish with mint leaves, if desired.

Makes 6 servings.

NOTE: Add crème de cassis when the syrup is cold; the flavor of the liqueur remains unaltered.

Kumquats in Cognac

1 lb. kumquats
1-1/4 cups water
1-1/2 cups sugar
2/3 cup cognac

Sterilize 2 or 3 small glass jars and lids and keep warm. Remove stalks and wash kumquats thoroughly. Dry on paper towels. Place water in a medium-sized saucepan. Add 1/2 cup sugar and heat gently, stirring occasionally, until sugar has dissolved. Bring to a boil.

Add kumquats and cook very gently 3 to 4 minutes, taking care kumquats do not split open. Remove kumquats with a slotted spoon and place on a plate. Place kumquats carefully in warm jars, without packing them too tightly, to neck of jar. Measure 2/3 cup of remaining syrup. Place in saucepan with remaining sugar. Stir over a gentle heat until sugar has dissolved.

Boil rapidly 1 minute until syrupy. Test by placing a drop of syrup between 2 cold teaspoons. Press together, then pull apart—a fine thread of sugar should form. Pour sugar syrup into a measuring cup and add same amount of cognac. Stir well and fill each jar to brim with cognac syrup. Seal jars with lids, label and store in a cool place up to 1 month. Makes 2 to 3 jars.

Steamed Fruit Dessert

12 ounces mixed fresh or frozen fruit such as
    black currants, plums and gooseberries,
    thawed if frozen
1/2 cup superfine sugar
1-1/2 cups self-rising flour
2 teaspoons baking powder
Pinch of salt
1 tablespoon butter
About 1/3 cup of milk
1 recipe Creme a la Vanilla, page 91, or
    Mousseline Sauce, page 90
Fresh mint to garnish, if desired

Grease a 5-cup bowl. Drain fruit and place in
greased bowl.

Add 1/2 of sugar to fruit (add a little more if
using tart fruit such as gooseberries). Sift
flour, baking powder and salt into a large
bowl and stir in remaining sugar. Cut in butter with fingertips until incorporated into dry
ingredients. Add milk and stir to form a soft
dough. Turn out onto a lightly floured surface, and pat to a circle to fit top of bowl; place
on top of fruit.

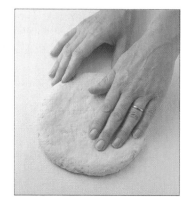

Cover bowl with a piece of foil, pleated in
middle. Tie securely around rim of bowl. Set
bowl in a saucepan of gently boiling water to
come halfway up sides and steam 1-1/2 hours.
Check water in pan occasionally and add
more boiling water, if necessary. Meanwhile,
prepare Crème à la Vanille or Mousseline
Sauce as directed. Garnish dessert with fresh
mint, if desired. Serve hot with sauce.

Makes 4 servings.

Pears in Dessert Wine

2 medium-size pears
1-1/4 cups sweet dessert wine
1/2 orange
1/2 lemon
1/4 cup superfine sugar
Whipping cream to decorate, if desired

Using a vegetable peeler, peel pears, leaving
stalks intact. Cut out as much core as possible
from flower end. In a small saucepan, lay
pears on their sides; they should fit snugly.
Pour dessert wine over pears.

Thinly peel orange and lemon, then cut peel
in julienne strips. Squeeze juice from orange
and lemon. Add peel, juices and sugar to
pears. Poach pears, covered, over low heat
until just tender.

Remove with a slotted spoon to a bowl. Cover
with cooking liquid, cool and chill 2 hours. In
a saucepan, boil cooking liquid vigorously until syrupy and reduced by half. Place pears on
individual serving plates and pour syrup over
pears. Decorate syrup with dabs of whipping
cream, if desired.

Makes 2 servings.

NOTE: Use leftover wine to pour over dried
fruit. Keep in a covered container. The fruit
will plump up and give flavor to fruit cakes
and puddings.

Summer Puddings

8 ounces red currants
8 ounces black currants
Juice of 1/2 orange
1/2 cup superfine sugar
1-2/3 cups fresh raspberries
12 to 16 thin slices white bread
Additional red currants to garnish, if desired

In a saucepan, combine currants, orange juice and sugar. Cook over low heat, stirring occasionally, until currants are juicy and just tender. Gently stir in 1-2/3 cups raspberries; cool.

Cut crusts from bread. From 6 slices, line 6 ramekin dishes or dariole molds, overlapping bread to line dishes completely. From remaining bread, cut circles same size as top of small ramekin dishes or dariole molds. Strain fruit, reserving juice, and spoon fruit into bread-lined dishes, pressing down quite firmly. Cover with bread circles. Pour some of reserved juice into dishes to soak bread. Place a small weight on top of each pudding.

Chill puddings and remaining juice several hours or overnight. To serve, turn puddings out onto individual plates and spoon a small amount of reserved juices over them. Garnish with additional red currants, if desired.

Makes 6 servings.

NOTE: A dariole mold is a small cylindrical mold used for cooking pastries or vegetables.

Banana Brûlée

Few crumbled Meringues, page 30, if desired
2-1/2 cups whipping cream
3 large bananas
Juice of 1 small lemon
1/4 cup superfine sugar
1/2 cup granulated sugar
1 tablespoon water

Prepare meringues, if desired, according to directions. In a large bowl, whip cream until thick. Slice bananas thinly into a separate bowl and toss in lemon juice.

Fold crumbled meringues, if desired, bananas and superfine sugar into whipped cream. Spoon mixture into a serving dish and chill.

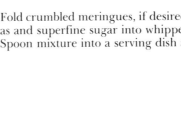

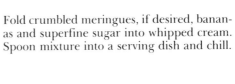

In a small saucepan, combine granulated sugar and water. Cook over low heat until sugar dissolves; do not stir. When sugar has dissolved, increase heat and boil syrup to a rich brown caramel. Immediately pour caramel in a thin stream over banana cream mixture and chill until caramel hardens. Serve within 1 to 2 hours.

Makes 6 servings.

Flaming Fruit Salad

Tropical Fruit with Mango Cream

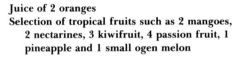

1 pound mixed dried fruit such as prunes,
   apricots, figs, apples, pears and peaches
   (7-1/2 cups)
2-1/2 cups water
2 tablespoons sherry
Juice of 1/2 lemon
2 tablespoons honey
1/2 (3-inch) cinnamon stick
1/4 cup brandy
3/4 cup toasted sliced almonds
1/2 cup walnuts, coarsely chopped
Fresh herbs to garnish, if desired

Soak dried fruit overnight in water and sherry.

Juice of 2 oranges
Selection of tropical fruits such as 2 mangoes,
   2 nectarines, 3 kiwifruit, 4 passion fruit, 1
   pineapple and 1 small ogen melon

Mango Cream:
1 large ripe mango
Juice of 1/2 orange
1 tablespoon kirsch, if desired
Squeeze of lemon juice
1 tablespoon superfine sugar
1 cup whipping cream

Strain orange juice into a glass measure.

In a saucepan, place fruit and soaking liquid, lemon juice, honey and cinnamon stick. Cover and simmer over low heat until fruit is just tender. Discard cinnamon stick, transfer fruit to a serving dish and keep warm.

To prepare fruit, peel mangoes, discard pit and slice. Cut nectarines in half, remove pit and slice. Peel kiwifruit and slice crosswise thinly. Cut passion fruit, but leave pulp in shells. Cut pineapple in half, discard leaves or use to decorate serving plate; peel, core and slice. Cut melon in half, discard seeds, peel and slice. Arrange fruit on a serving plate.

In a small pan, heat brandy and light. While still flaming, pour over fruit and sprinkle with almonds and walnuts. Garnish with fresh herbs, if desired, and serve immediately.

Makes 5 to 6 servings.

NOTE: The effect of flaming brandy is to burn off the alcohol and so concentrate the flavor. It is important to warm brandy first or it will not light.

Sprinkle fruit with orange juice, cover with plastic wrap and chill until ready to serve. To prepare mango cream, peel mango and discard pit. In a blender or food processor fitted with the metal blade, process pulp, orange juice, kirsch, if desired, and lemon juice to a puree. Fold in sugar. In a bowl, whip cream until stiff, then using a knife to give a marbled effect, fold whipped cream into puree. Serve mango cream with tropical fruit platter.

Makes 6 servings.

Lime & Tangerine Gâteau

3 eggs, separated
2 (4-oz.) pkgs. cream cheese, softened
1/2 cup superfine sugar
Finely grated peel and juice 2 tangerines
Finely grated peel and juice 2 limes
1 tablespoon plus 2 teaspoons plain gelatin
3 tablespoons water
1 pound cake
2/3 cup whipping cream
3 tablespoons fromage frais
1/4 cup chopped pistachio nuts
Lime and tangerine wedges to decorate

To prepare filling, beat egg yolks, cream cheese and sugar in a bowl with a wooden spoon until smooth. Stir in grated fruit peel and 1/2 of juices.

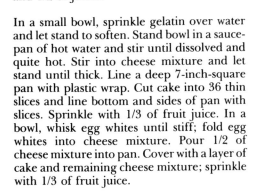

In a small bowl, sprinkle gelatin over water and let stand to soften. Stand bowl in a saucepan of hot water and stir until dissolved and quite hot. Stir into cheese mixture and let stand until thick. Line a deep 7-inch-square pan with plastic wrap. Cut cake into 36 thin slices and line bottom and sides of pan with slices. Sprinkle with 1/3 of fruit juice. In a bowl, whisk egg whites until stiff; fold egg whites into cheese mixture. Pour 1/2 of cheese mixture into pan. Cover with a layer of cake and remaining cheese mixture; sprinkle with 1/3 of fruit juice.

Top with remaining cake and fruit juice. Cover with plastic wrap and chill until set; leave in pan until required. Remove gâteau from pan and remove plastic wrap carefully. In a bowl, whip cream and fromage frais until thick. Spoon 1/4 of mixture into a pastry bag fitted with a small star nozzle. Spread remaining cream evenly over gâteau and press pistachio nuts onto all sides to coat evenly. Pipe a shell border around top of gâteau and decorate with fruit wedges. Makes 12 servings.

Orange-Strawberry Romanoff

1-1/2 pounds fresh strawberries, hulled
Grated peel of 1 orange
1 tablespoon plus 1 teaspoon Grand Marnier
1-1/4 cups whipping cream
2 tablespoons crème fraîche
1 to 2 tablespoons powdered sugar
Cookies to serve

Reserve 4 strawberries and slice remainder into a bowl. Add orange peel and Grand Marnier. Gently mix, then let stand 15 minutes.

In a bowl, whip cream until quite stiff, then fold in crème fraîche. Sift powdered sugar over whipped cream and fold in. Place 1 spoonful of strawberries into each of 4 dessert dishes. Mash remainder gently and fold into whipped cream mixture.

Carefully spoon mixture over strawberries in glasses and chill until ready to serve. Decorate with reserved strawberries, cut in fan shapes. Serve with cookies.

Makes 4 servings.

NOTE: Keep strawberries in a colander. The air circulating around them helps to keep them fresh. Do not hull strawberries until ready to eat.

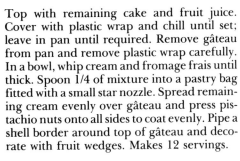

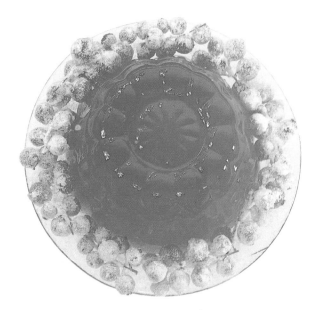

Tart Lemon Mold

2-1/2 cups milk
1/3 cup granulated sugar
1 (1/4-oz.) envelope unflavored gelatin
    (1 tablespoon)
3 small egg yolks
Grated peel and juice of 1 large lemon
1/3 cup superfine sugar
Twists of lemon and fresh herbs to garnish, if
    desired

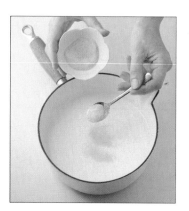

In a small saucepan, combine milk, granulated sugar and gelatin. Cook over low heat, stirring constantly, until almost to boiling point; do not boil. Remove from heat.

In a bowl, beat egg yolks lightly. Gradually pour hot milk over beaten egg yolks, stirring constantly. Pour into a 3-3/4-cup mold. Chill until set.

Meanwhile, in a small saucepan, combine grated lemon peel and juice with superfine sugar and stir over low heat until sugar dissolves; cool. To serve, turn out mold onto a serving plate and pour cold lemon syrup around mold. Garnish with lemon twists and fresh herbs, if desired.

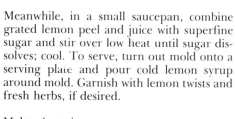

Makes 4 servings.

Port Gelatin with Frosted Fruit

Peel and juice of 1/2 orange
Peel and juice of 1 lemon
2-1/2 cups ruby port
1/3 cup superfine sugar
1 (3-inch) cinnamon stick
1-2/3 (1/4-oz.) envelopes unflavored gelatin
    (1 tablespoon plus 2 teaspoons)

Frosted Fruit:
1 egg white
Small bunches of red currants and seedless
    grapes
Superfine sugar

Using a vegetable peeler, thinly peel orange and lemon. In a saucepan, combine fruit peel, port, lemon juice and squeezed lemon shell.

Add sugar and cinnamon stick and heat gently until sugar dissolves. Let stand 20 minutes to infuse. In a small bowl, sprinkle gelatin into orange juice and let stand 2 to 3 minutes, until softened. Set bowl of gelatin in a saucepan of hot water and stir until dissolved. Stir gelatin into port, then strain mixture through a fine sieve into a wetted 3-1/4-cup mold.

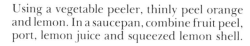

Chill until set. To prepare frosted fruit, lightly whisk egg white in a shallow dish. Wash and dry fruit. Dip into whisked egg white and then into sugar to coat thoroughly. Place on waxed paper to dry. To serve, turn out mold onto a serving dish and decorate with frosted fruit.

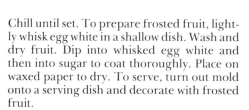

Makes 4 to 6 servings.

CHOCOLATE DESSERTS

Molded Chocolate Pudding

9 ounces semisweet chocolate
1/4 cup plus 1 tablespoon strong coffee
12 tablespoons unsalted butter, diced
3/4 cup superfine sugar
4 large eggs, beaten
1-1/2 cups whipping cream
Tiny edible flowers to decorate, if desired

Preheat oven to 350F (175C). Line a 4-cup bowl or soufflé dish with a double thickness of foil.

In top of a double boiler or bowl set over a pan of simmering water, melt chocolate with coffee. Gradually beat in butter and sugar and heat until mixture is hot and butter melts. Remove from heat and gradually whisk in eggs. Strain mixture into prepared dish, cover with foil and place in a roasting pan. Add enough boiling water to pan to come halfway up dish. Bake 1 hour, until top has a thick crust. Cool, then refrigerate.

To serve, unmold pudding onto a serving dish and carefully peel away foil; pudding is rich and sticky. In a bowl, whip cream until stiff, then cover pudding with 2/3 of whipped cream. Using a pastry bag fitted with a star nozzle, pipe remaining whipped cream in rosettes around top and bottom of pudding. Decorate with flowers, if desired.

Makes 6 to 8 servings.

Chocolate Trifle

3-1/2 ounces semisweet chocolate
2 tablespoons rum
2 tablespoons water
4 egg yolks
1 tablespoon superfine sugar
3 cups whipping cream
8 ounces plain or trifle sponge cakes
1/2 cup apricot jam
12 ounces mixed fruit such as grapes, ripe
    pears and bananas
Grated semisweet chocolate to decorate, if
    desired

In top of a double boiler or a bowl set over a saucepan of simmering water, melt chocolate with rum and water.

In a large bowl, whisk egg yolks and sugar until light and fluffy. In a saucepan, bring whipping cream almost to boiling point. Whisk into egg yolk mixture with melted chocolate mixture. Return mixture to saucepan and whisk over a very low heat until chocolate is incorporated and mixture has thickened slightly. Slice sponge cakes in half. In a small saucepan warm jam slightly and brush over sponge cakes.

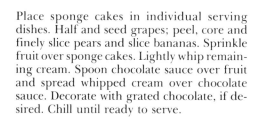

Place sponge cakes in individual serving dishes. Half and seed grapes; peel, core and finely slice pears and slice bananas. Sprinkle fruit over sponge cakes. Lightly whip remaining cream. Spoon chocolate sauce over fruit and spread whipped cream over chocolate sauce. Decorate with grated chocolate, if desired. Chill until ready to serve.

Makes 6 servings.

Chocolate Pears

2 ounces amaretti cookies (macaroons)
3 to 4 tablespoons Cointreau
4 ounces semisweet chocolate
3 tablespoons strong coffee
1 tablespoon orange juice
2 tablespoons butter
2 eggs, separated
4 ripe medium-size pears
Orange peel curls and fresh mint to garnish, if desired

Place amaretti cookies in a bowl. Pour liqueur over cookies. Using end of a rolling pin, crush cookies to rough crumbs.

In top of a double boiler or a bowl set over a pan of simmering water, melt chocolate with coffee and orange juice, stirring until smooth. Remove from heat and beat in butter and egg yolks. In a separate bowl, whisk egg whites until stiff and fold chocolate mixture into them. Set aside. Peel pears, leaving them whole with stems in tact. Hollow out as much core as possible from bottom and fill cavity with crumb mixture.

Set pears on a wire rack, cutting off a small slice to make them stand upright, if necessary. Spoon chocolate mixture over pears to coat evenly. Chill several hours or overnight. To serve, place on individual plates. Garnish with orange peel and mint, if desired.

Makes 4 servings.

Rich Chocolate Log

1 (14-oz.) can sweetened condensed milk
3 ounces semisweet chocolate
3 tablespoons butter
1 pound plain sponge cake
2/3 cup glacé cherries, halved
1/2 cup walnuts, chopped
3 tablespoons chopped pitted dates

Chocolate Fudge Icing:
3 tablespoons butter
1/4 cup superfine sugar
2 tablespoons water
1/2 cup powdered sugar
1/4 cup unsweetened cocoa powder

Glacé cherries, cut in strips, and walnut halves to garnish, if desired

In a saucepan, combine milk, chocolate and butter. Stir over low heat until chocolate and butter have melted and ingredients are well combined. Remove from heat. In a blender or food processor fitted with the metal blade, process cake to crumbs. Stir crumbs into chocolate mixture. Stir in cherries, walnuts and dates. Spoon mixture onto a large piece of waxed paper and form in a log shape. Roll up in waxed paper. Chill overnight.

Two hours before serving, unwrap log and place on a serving dish. To prepare icing, in a saucepan, combine butter, superfine sugar and water. Bring to a boil. Sift powdered sugar and cocoa into pan and beat well. Cool until fudgy, then spread over roll. Mark lines along roll with a fork. Garnish with glacé sherry strips and walnut halves, if desired.

Makes 8 to 10 servings.

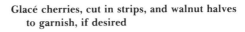

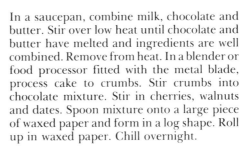

Gâteau Grenoble

1/3 cup hazelnuts, skinned
4 eggs, separated, plus 1 extra white
1/2 cup plus 1 tablespoon superfine sugar
3 ounces semisweet chocolate
2-1/2 cups walnuts, finely chopped
Whipped cream to serve
Additional chopped walnuts and mint leaves to
  garnish, if desired

Preheat oven to 300F (150C). Generously butter an 8" x 4" loaf pan. Grind hazelnuts in a coffee grinder. In a large bowl, beat egg yolks, then gradually beat in 1/2 cup of sugar, until mixture is light and fluffy.

In top of a double boiler or a bowl set over a pan of simmering water, melt chocolate and stir into yolk mixture with hazelnuts and walnuts. In a large bowl, whisk egg whites until stiff but not dry. Sprinkle in remaining sugar and whisk again until mixture is glossy; fold 2 to 3 tablespoons into chocolate mixture.

Carefully fold remaining egg white into chocolate mixture. (This is quite hard to do as chocolate mixture is very stiff; keep cutting and folding until it is incorporated.) Pour into buttered pan and place in a roasting pan. Add boiling water to come halfway up dish. Cover and bake 1-1/2 hours; cool. Slice and serve with whipped cream. Sprinkle additional chopped walnuts on whipped cream and garnish with mint leaves, if desired.

Makes 6 servings.

Chocolate & Chestnut Gâteau

12 tablespoons butter, softened
1/2 cup superfine sugar
6 ounces semisweet chocolate
3 tablespoons strong coffee
1 (14-oz.) can unsweetened chestnut puree
1-1/4 cups whipping cream

Oil an 8" x 4" loaf pan. In a bowl, cream butter and sugar until light and fluffy.

In top of a double boiler or bowl set over a pan of simmering water, melt chocolate with coffee. Add chestnut puree and melted chocolate to creamed butter and beat until smooth. Spoon mixture into oiled pan and level surface. Cover with foil and freeze 3 hours.

Turn out onto a serving plate. In a bowl, whip cream until stiff. Using a pastry bag fitted with a star nozzle, pipe rosettes of whipped cream on top. Let gâteau stand 30 minutes at room temperature to soften before serving.

Makes 6 to 8 servings.

Chocolate Ring Cake

3 ounces semisweet chocolate
4 tablespoons unsalted butter
2 to 3 tablespoons strong coffee
3/4 cup superfine sugar
1 egg, separated, plus 1 extra white
1/2 teaspoon baking soda
1/3 cup whipping cream
1-1/4 cups all-purpose flour
1/2 teaspoon baking powder

Chocolate Frosting:
4 ounces semisweet chocolate
2/3 cup whipping cream
4 tablespoons butter
1 cup powdered sugar
Few drops vanilla extract

White chocolate leaves and tiny edible flowers to decorate, if desired

Preheat oven to 350F (175C). Grease a 5-cup savarin or ring mold and dust with flour. In top of a double boiler or a bowl set over a pan of simmering water, melt chocolate with butter and coffee. Add sugar and stir until sugar dissolves.

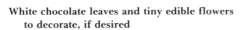
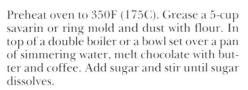

In a bowl, beat egg yolk, baking soda and whipping cream, then stir into chocolate. Sift flour and baking powder into chocolate mixture and fold together.

In a medium-size bowl, whisk egg whites until stiff but not dry. Add 1 tablespoon to chocolate mixture, then pour chocolate mixture over egg whites and fold together. Pour into prepared pan and bake 45 to 50 minutes, until set and spongy to touch. Cool cake in pan.

To make frosting, in a small saucepan, combine all ingredients and cook over very gentle heat, stirring constantly, until chocolate and butter have melted and ingredients are thoroughly combined.

Turn out cake onto a wire rack. Quickly pour frosting over cake and decorate with chocolate leaves and tiny flowers, if desired. Serve immediately.

Makes 10 servings.

VARIATIONS: Omit decorations and sprinkle with 2 tablespoons toasted sliced almonds; the nuts give a crunchy texture. Omit frosting and serve with Dark Chocolate Sauce, page 92.

White & Dark Chocolate Terrine

White Chocolate Mousse:
9 ounces white chocolate
1/2 (1/4-oz.) envelope unflavored gelatin
(1-1/2 teaspoons)
5 tablespoons water
1 tablespoon light corn syrup
2 egg yolks
2/3 cup whipping cream
2/3 cup dairy sour cream

Dark Chocolate Mousse:
6 ounces semisweet chocolate
1/4 cup strong coffee
2/3 (1/4-oz.) envelope unflavored gelatin
(2 teaspoons)
3 tablespoons water
8 tablespoons butter, cubed
2 egg yolks
1-1/4 cups whipping cream

Whipped cream and grated semisweet
chocolate to decorate, if desired

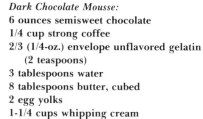

Line an 8" x 4" loaf pan with plastic wrap to overlap edges. To prepare white chocolate mousse, break white chocolate in small pieces and set aside. In a small bowl, sprinkle gelatin over 2 tablespoons of water and let stand 2 to 3 minutes, until softened. In a saucepan, combine remaining water and corn syrup and bring to boil. Remove from heat and stir in gelatin until dissolved. Add chocolate pieces and beat until chocolate is melted and mixture is smooth.

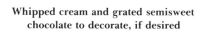

Beat in egg yolks, 1 at a time. In a bowl, whip whipping cream and sour cream lightly and fold into chocolate mixture. Pour into prepared loaf pan and refrigerate until set.

To prepare dark chocolate mousse, in top of a double boiler or bowl set over a pan of simmering water, melt chocolate with coffee. In a small bowl, sprinkle gelatin over water and let stand 2 to 3 minutes, until softened. Set bowl of gelatin in a saucepan of hot water and stir until dissolved. Stir gelatin and butter into chocolate mixture and beat until butter has melted and mixture is smooth. Cool, then beat in egg yolks. In a bowl, whip cream lightly and fold into chocolate mixture.

Pour dark chocolate mixture over set white chocolate mousse. Refrigerate until set, then cover with overlapping plastic wrap and refrigerate overnight.

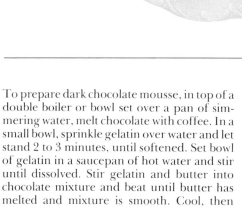

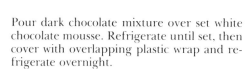

To serve, unfold plastic wrap from top and turn out onto a serving dish. Carefully peel off plastic wrap. Decorate with whipped cream and grated chocolate, if desired, and cut in slices.

Makes 8 to 10 servings.

Saucy Chocolate Pudding

3 (1-oz.) squares white chocolate
3 (1-oz.) squares milk chocolate
3 (1-oz.) squares semi-sweet chocolate
3 egg yolks
2 teaspoons finely grated grapefruit peel
2 teaspoons grapefruit juice
1 tablespoon ginger wine
1 tablespoon Southern Comfort liqueur
3/4 cup softened butter
2/3 cup whipping cream
3 tablespoons fromage frais
Grapefuit slices and mint sprigs to decorate

Grapefruit Sauce:
Finely grated peel and juice 1 grapefruit
Water
2 teaspoons cornstarch
1 tablespoon superfine sugar

Break up each chocolate and place in separate bowls. Set each over a saucepan of hand-hot water. Stir occasionally until melted and smooth. Stir an egg yolk into each. Stir grapefruit peel and juice into white chocolate, ginger wine into milk chocolate and Southern Comfort into semi-sweet chocolate until smooth. Let stand until cold. Beat butter until light and fluffy. Whip cream until thick. Add 1/3 of each to chocolate mixtures and fold in until smooth and evenly blended. Line 6 individual molds with plastic wrap. Divide milk chocolate mixture between molds, making 1 layer.

Repeat with white chocolate layer and finally semi-sweet chocolate layer. Tap molds to level and freeze until firm or until needed. To prepare sauce, measure grapefruit juice and peel and enough water to measure 3/4 cup. Blend juice, cornstarch and sugar. Bring to a boil, stirring constantly. Cook gently 30 seconds; cool. Invert molds 20 minutes before serving. Pour grapefruit sauce around bottom. Decorate with grapefruit and mint. Makes 6 servings.

Strawberry Chocolate Boxes

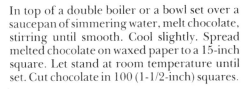

1 pound semisweet chocolate
1 recipe Whisked Sponge Cake made with 3
    eggs, 1/3 cup superfine sugar and 3/4 cup
    self-rising flour, page 68
3 to 4 tablespoons strawberry jam, sieved
1 cup whipping cream
Superfine sugar to taste
1-2/3 cups fresh strawberries
Tiny edible flowers to garnish, if desired

In top of a double boiler or a bowl set over a saucepan of simmering water, melt chocolate, stirring until smooth. Cool slightly. Spread melted chocolate on waxed paper to a 15-inch square. Let stand at room temperature until set. Cut chocolate in 100 (1-1/2-inch) squares.

Prepare cake according to recipe. Bake in an 8-inch square pan and cool. Cut cake in 16 (1-1/2-inch) squares, trimming as necessary. Reserve remainder for another use. In a small saucepan, warm jam slightly, then brush jam lightly all over cake squares. Place each cake square on a chocolate square. Press 4 more chocolate squares around sides.

In a bowl, whip cream to stiff peaks and sweeten with sugar. Slice strawberries, if desired. Carefully spoon whipped cream on top of each box, then cover with strawberries. Place a chocolate square on top of each box to make a lid. Chill and serve within 1 to 2 hours. Garnish with tiny flowers, if desired.

Makes 16 boxes.

White & Dark Chocolate Pots

4 (1-oz.) squares white chocolate
4 (1-oz.) squares semi-sweet chocolate
4 eggs, separated
1 tablespoon rum
1 tablespoon Cointreau liqueur
Orange peel spirals to decorate

Break up each chocolate and place in a separate bowl. Set each over a saucepan of hand-hot water. Stir occasionally until melted and smooth. Stir 2 egg yolks into each. Stir rum into semi-sweet chocolate and Cointreau into white chocolate until evenly blended.

In a bowl, stiffly beat egg whites. Add 1/2 to each chocolate mixture. Fold in carefully until each mixture is evenly blended and smooth.

Spoon alternate spoonfuls of each mixture evenly into 8 small dessert dishes. Leave in a cool place to set. Decorate with orange peel spirals. Makes 8 servings.

Chocolate Mousse Cups

5 ounces white chocolate
Grated peel and juice of 1 orange
1/2 (1/4-oz.) envelope unflavored gelatin
   (1-1/2 teaspoons)
2 eggs, separated
3/4 cup whipping cream
1/2 cup dairy sour cream
Shredded orange peel and tiny edible flowers
   to decorate, if desired

Chocolate Cups:
12 ounces semisweet chocolate
3 tablespoons butter

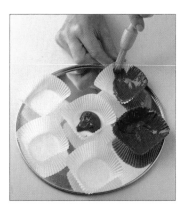

To prepare chocolate cups, in top of a double boiler or bowl set over pan of simmering water, melt semisweet chocolate. Stir in butter. Using a pastry brush, brush chocolate over bottom and sides of 12 paper cups. Chill until hardened.

Meanwhile, to prepare mousse, in top of a double boiler or bowl set over pan of simmering water, melt white chocolate with 1/2 of orange juice. In a small bowl, sprinkle gelatin over remaining orange juice and let stand 2 to 3 minutes, until softened. Set bowl of gelatin in a saucepan of hot water and stir until dissolved. Stir into chocolate mixture with orange peel; cool.

Beat egg yolks into cooled chocolate mixture. In a bowl, whip cream and sour cream. In a separate bowl, whisk egg whites until stiff. Fold whipped creams, then egg whites into chocolate mixture and chill until almost set. Spoon mousse into chocolate cups and refrigerate until mousse has set. Peel away paper cups before serving. Decorate with orange peel and flowers, if desired.

Makes 12 servings.

CAKE DESSERTS

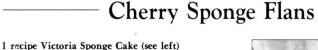

Victoria Sponge Cake

8 tablespoons margarine or butter, softened
1/2 cup superfine sugar
2 large eggs, beaten
1 cup self-rising flour
Milk, if necessary
Whipped cream and sliced strawberries and
    kiwifruit to serve
Additional strawberries and leaves to garnish,
    if desired

Preheat oven to 350F (175C). Grease 2 (8-inch) round cake pans.

In a bowl, cream margarine and sugar until light and fluffy. Beat eggs into creamed margarine and sugar, a little at a time. Sift flour into mixture and fold in, using a metal spoon. Mixture should be a soft dropping consistency; add a little milk, if necessary. Spoon into greased pan. Bake about 20 to 25 minutes, until golden and spongy to touch. Turn out and cool on a wire rack.

Spread 1/2 of whipped cream on top of 1 cake and arrange 1/2 of fruit on whipped cream. Top with remaining cake. Spread or pipe remaining whipped cream on top of cake and arrange remaining fruit on whipped cream. Garnish with additional strawberries and leaves, if desired.

Makes 6 servings.

VARIATION: Flavor with a few drops of vanilla extract or 1 tablespoon grated orange or lemon peel. Beat into mixture before adding flour.

Cherry Sponge Flans

1 recipe Victoria Sponge Cake (see left)
1 pound fresh sweet dark cherries, pitted
1 tablespoon superfine sugar
1 teaspoon arrowroot
1 tablespoon water
1 tablespoon kirsch
1-1/4 cups whipping cream
Fresh sweet cherries and mint leaves to
    garnish, if desired

Preheat oven to 350F (175C). Grease 8 individual 4-inch pans, then dust with sugar and flour. Prepare sponge cake as directed. Divide among greased pans and bake 5 to 10 minutes, until golden and spongy to touch.

Cool in pans. In a saucepan, combine cherries and sugar. Cover and cook over low heat until juices run. Mix arrowroot and water to a smooth paste and stir into cherries. Bring to a boil, stirring constantly, then remove from heat; cool. Stir in kirsch.

To serve, place sponge cakes on individual serving plates. In a bowl, whip cream until stiff and spread over sponge cakes. Spoon cherries and sauce over whipped cream. Using a pastry bag fitted with a star nozzle, pipe a border of whipped cream around cherries. Garnish with fresh cherries and mint leaves, if desired, and serve immediately.

Makes 8 servings.

Hot Orange Cake

8 tablespoons butter, softened
1/2 cup superfine sugar
2 large eggs, separated
1 cup self-rising flour
Grated peel and juice of 3 small oranges
1 cup whipping cream
Powdered sugar and fresh orange sections to decorate

Preheat oven to 350F (175C). In a large bowl, cream butter and superfine sugar until light and fluffy. Beat egg yolks into mixture with 1 tablespoon of flour and grated peel and juice of 1 orange.

In a separate bowl, whisk egg whites until stiff but not dry; fold into creamed mixture with remaining flour. Spoon into a deep 8-inch nonstick cake pan. Bake 20 to 30 minutes, until golden-brown and springy to touch.

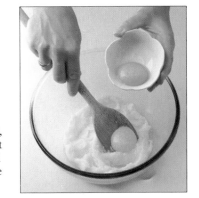

Meanwhile, in a bowl, whip cream and remaining orange juice and peel until stiff. Leave cake in pan 2 to 3 minutes, then turn out and cut in half crosswise. Working quickly, spread bottom with whipped cream and cover with top half of cake. Dust thickly with powdered sugar and arrange orange sections on top. Serve at once.

Makes 6 servings.

NOTE: The whipped cream will melt, so serve as quickly as possible.

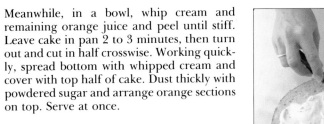

Coffee-Brandy Cake

1 recipe Victoria Sponge Cake (see opposite)
2 tablespoons brandy
1 tablespoon superfine sugar
1-1/4 cups hot strong coffee
1-1/4 cups whipping cream
1 tablespoon powdered sugar
1/2 cup sliced almonds, toasted

Prepare sponge cake as directed and bake in a 2-1/2-cup greased bowl. Cool in bowl.

When cake is cold, stir brandy and superfine sugar into hot coffee and pour over cake while still in bowl. Place a saucer over bowl and chill overnight.

About 2 hours before serving, run a knife around edges of cake, then turn out on a serving plate. In a bowl, whip cream and powdered sugar until very stiff and spread evenly over cake, covering completely; chill. Just before serving, stick toasted almonds into surface of whipped cream all over cake.

Makes 4 to 6 servings.

VARIATION: Using a pastry bag fitted with a star nozzle, pipe rosettes of whipped cream all over cake and decorate with sliced almonds and tiny edible flowers.

Berry-Filled Cake

Whisked Sponge Cake:
6 eggs
3/4 cup superfine sugar
Finely grated peel of 1 lemon or small orange
1-1/2 cups self-rising flour

Filling:
1-1/4 cups whipping cream
1 tablespoon kirsch
Superfine sugar to taste
8 ounces raspberries
1 pound strawberries

Powdered sugar
Red currants to garnish, if desired

Preheat oven to 350F (175C). Grease a 9-inch-square baking pan and dust with sugar and then flour; this gives a sugary coating to sides of cake.

To prepare sponge cake, in a large bowl, whisk eggs, sugar and lemon or orange peel until very thick, pale and mousse-like. If desired, set bowl over a pan of gently simmering water to help with whisking, but continue to whisk until mixture is cold.

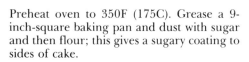

Sift flour twice onto a plate, then carefully, but thoroughly, fold into egg mixture. Spoon into greased pan. Bake 12 to 15 minutes, until lightly golden and springy to touch. Cool on a wire rack.

To prepare filling, in a large bowl, whip cream until stiff and fold in kirsch and sugar. Fold in 1/2 of raspberries. Slice strawberries and set aside with remaining raspberries.

Cut cool sponge cake horizontally through center. Put bottom half on a serving dish. Cut a square out of center of remaining half to leave a 1 inch unbroken frame.

Place frame exactly on top of cake half. Fill frame with whipped cream mixture and top with sliced strawberries and remaining raspberries. Cut remaining piece of sponge cake diagonally in half and set on top like butterfly wings. Dust with powdered sugar. Serve within 1 hour. Garnish with red currants, if desired.

Makes 8 servings.

Variation: Decorate cake with whipped cream, toasted sliced almonds and strawberry slices.

Rum Truffle Cake

7 (1-oz.) squares semi-sweet chocolate
1/2 cup unsalted butter
1/4 cup dark rum
3 eggs, separated
1/2 cup superfine sugar
3/4 cup all-purpose flour
1/2 cup ground almonds

Filling & Icing:
7 (1-oz.) squares semi-sweet chocolate
1-1/4 cups whipping cream
1 tablespoon dark rum
2 (1-oz.) squares white chocolate, grated

In a bowl, whisk egg whites until stiff. Fold 1/3 at a time into chocolate mixture until all egg whites are incorporated. Pour mixture into prepared pan. Bake in oven 45 to 55 minutes or until firm to touch in center. Turn out of pan and cool on a wire rack.

Preheat oven to 350F (175C). Butter and flour a 2-1/2-inch deep 8-inch-round cake pan. Line bottom with a circle of waxed paper.

Place chocolate and butter in a bowl over hand-hot water. Stir occasionally until melted. Add rum and stir well.

To prepare filling, melt 4 squares of chocolate with 1/4 cup of whipping cream in a bowl set over hot water. Stir in rum until well blended. Let stand until cool. To prepare icing, whip 1/2 cup of whipping cream in a bowl until thick. Add 1/2 of rum-chocolate to whipped cream and fold in until smooth.

Place egg yolks and sugar in a bowl over a saucepan of simmering water. Whisk until thick and pale. Remove bowl from saucepan. Continue to whisk until mixture leaves a trail when whisk has been lifted. Stir chocolate mixture into egg yolk mixture until evenly blended. In a small bowl, mix flour and ground almonds. Add to chocolate mixture; fold in carefully using a spatula.

Cut cake in half. Sandwich together with chocolate icing and spread remainder over top and sides. Chill cake and remaining rum-chocolate mixture in bowl. Melt remaining chocolate with whipping cream in a bowl set over hot water. Stir until smooth and cool until thick. Spread chocolate mixture over cake to cover evenly. Shape rum-chocolate mixture into 16 truffles. Coat in grated white chocolate. Arrange truffles on top of cake and chill to set. Makes 10 servings.

Griestorte

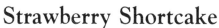

3 eggs, separated
1/3 cup plus 1 tablespoon superfine sugar
Grated peel of 1 orange
Juice of 1/2 lemon
1/3 cup fine semolina
1/4 cup ground almonds
1 cup whipping cream
1-3/4 cups raspberries
Powdered sugar
Mint leaves to garnish, if desired

Preheat oven to 350F (175C). In a bowl, beat egg yolks, superfine sugar and orange peel until light and fluffy.

Beat in lemon juice, semolina and ground almonds. In a separate bowl, whisk egg whites until stiff, then fold into almond mixture. Pour into a deep 8-inch nonstick cake pan and bake 35 minutes, until golden-brown and firm to touch. Turn out of pan and cool on a wire rack. In a bowl, whip cream until stiff. Cut cold cake in half crosswise and spread bottom half with 1/2 of whipped cream.

Arrange raspberries over whipped cream, reserving a few for decoration. Top with remaining cake half. Dust top with powdered sugar. Using a pastry bag fitted with a star nozzle, pipe remaining whipped cream in a border of rosettes. Decorate with reserved raspberries and mint leaves, if desired.

Makes 6 servings.

NOTE: If desired, lay strips of waxed paper over cake in a lattice pattern. Dust with powdered sugar and remove strips.

Strawberry Shortcake

8 tablespoons butter, softened
1/4 cup superfine sugar
1-1/4 cups all-purpose flour
3 tablespoons cornstarch
2-1/4 cups strawberries, sliced
3 tablespoons red currant jelly
1-1/4 cups whipping cream
Additional sliced strawberries and mint leaves to garnish, if desired

In a bowl, cream butter and sugar until light and fluffy. Sift flour and cornstarch into creamy mixture and stir to make a firm dough.

Wrap in foil and chill 30 minutes. Preheat oven to 350F (175C). Place dough on a baking sheet and pat or roll to a circle about 1/2 inch thick. Prick all over with a fork and bake about 20 minutes, until lightly golden. Cool on baking sheet.

Carefully transfer shortcake to a serving plate and cover with whole strawberries. In a small saucepan, melt red currant jelly and brush over strawberries. In a bowl, whip cream until stiff. Using a pastry bag fitted with a star nozzle, pipe a border of whipped cream around edge of shortcake. Serve within 1 hour. Garnish with additional sliced strawberries and mint leaves, if desired.

Makes 6 to 8 servings.

Orange Roll

5 eggs, separated
3/4 cup superfine sugar
Grated peel and juice of 2 oranges
Powdered sugar
1-1/4 cups whipping cream
Additional superfine sugar to taste
Fresh orange sections and fresh herbs to
    garnish, if desired
1 recipe Raspberry Sauce, page 91, if desired

Preheat oven to 350F (175C). Line a jelly-roll pan with a double thickness of foil and grease generously. In a bowl, whisk egg yolks, 3/4 cup superfine sugar and orange peel until thick.

In a large bowl, whisk egg whites until stiff but not dry. Fold 1 tablespoon of whipped egg whites into egg yolk mixture, then pour egg yolk mixture onto whites and fold in carefully. Pour into prepared pan and spread evenly. Bake 30 minutes, remove from oven and immediately cover with a damp tea towel. When cold, turn onto a piece of foil dusted thickly with powdered sugar. Peel off bottom layer of foil, tearing in long thin strips.

In a bowl, whip cream lightly and sweeten to taste with additional superfine sugar. Add orange juice gradually, whisking constantly until stiff. Reserve a small amount of whipped cream for decoration and spread remainder evenly over sponge cake. Roll up, using foil to help, and transfer to a serving plate. Using a pastry bag fitted with a star nozzle, pipe rosettes of reserved whipped cream along sides of roll. Garnish with fresh orange sections and fresh herbs, if desired. Serve with Raspberry Sauce, if desired.

Makes 6 servings.

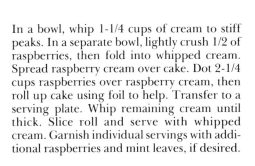

Raspberry & Hazelnut Roll

1-2/3 cups hazelnuts
5 eggs, separated
2/3 cup superfine sugar
Powdered sugar
1-3/4 cups whipping cream
2-1/4 cups raspberries
Additional raspberries and mint leaves to
    garnish, if desired

Preheat oven to 350F (175C). Line a jelly-roll pan with a double thickness of foil and oil thoroughly. In a food processor fitted with the metal blade, process hazelnuts until finely ground.

In a large bowl, whisk egg yolks and superfine sugar until thick and mousse-like. Fold in ground hazelnuts. In a separate bowl, whisk egg whites until stiff but not dry. Fold carefully into nut mixture, then pour into prepared pan and spread evenly. Bake 15 to 20 minutes, until risen and firm to touch. Cover immediately with a damp tea towel and let stand overnight. The next day, turn out cake onto a sheet of foil thickly dusted with powdered sugar. Peel off foil.

In a bowl, whip 1-1/4 cups of cream to stiff peaks. In a separate bowl, lightly crush 1/2 of raspberries, then fold into whipped cream. Spread raspberry cream over cake. Dot 2-1/4 cups raspberries over raspberry cream, then roll up cake using foil to help. Transfer to a serving plate. Whip remaining cream until thick. Slice roll and serve with whipped cream. Garnish individual servings with additional raspberries and mint leaves, if desired.

Makes 6 servings.

Chocolate Cherry Slice

Cake:
6 (1-oz.) squares semi-sweet chocolate
4 eggs
1/4 cup superfine sugar
1/3 cup all-purpose flour

Filling:
1 cup unsweetened marron purée
4 (1-oz.) squares semi-sweet chocolate, melted
1-1/4 cups whipping cream
3 tablespoons cherry jam
1 cup sweet cherries, pitted, halved

Preheat oven to 350F (175C). Line a 13" x 9" jelly roll pan with waxed paper. To prepare cake, break up chocolate; place in a bowl over a saucepan of hand-hot water. Stir occasionally until melted and smooth.

In a bowl, whisk eggs and sugar until thick and pale and a trail is left when whisk is lifted. Stir in chocolate until evenly blended. Sift in flour and fold in gently until evenly mixed. Pour mixture into prepared pan and shake to level. Bake in oven 20 to 25 minutes or until firm to touch. Remove from oven. Cover with a damp tea towel and let stand until cold. To prepare filling, process marron in a food processor fitted with a metal blade to a purée. Add chocolate and process until smooth. In a small bowl, whip cream until thick. Place 1/3 of whipped cream into a pastry bag fitted with small star nozzle. Fold remaining whipped cream into chocolate mixture.

Remove cake from pan. Remove paper, trim edges and cut into 3 short strips across width. Spread 2 strips of cake with jam. Cover each with 1/3 of filling. Spread smoothly. Arrange 1/3 of cherry halves on each and stack layers on a serving plate. Top with remaining cake layer. Spread top and sides of cake evenly with remaining filling and pipe scrolls of whipping cream around top edge. Decorate with remaining cherry halves. Chill until needed. Makes 10 servings.

Plum & Apple Kuchen

1 (6-oz.) pkg. pizza crust mix
Warm water
2 tablespoons butter, melted
3/4 cup ground almonds
1/4 cup superfine sugar
1 teaspoon ground mixed spice
1 lb. cooking apples, peeled, cored, sliced
2 lb. plums, pitted, halved
1/3 cup plum jam, boiled, sieved
1 tablespoon flaked almonds

Preheat oven to 425F (220C). Butter a flan pan or a baking sheet. Place pizza mix in a bowl. Add warm water as directed by instructions on packet. Knead dough until smooth. Cover and let stand for 5 minutes.

Re-knead dough and roll out to a 12-inch round on a lightly floured surface. Place in buttered flan pan or on baking sheet. Brush dough with butter. In a bowl, mix together almonds, sugar and mixed spice. Sprinkle over dough.

Arrange apple slices and plum halves in a circular pattern over almond mixture. Bake in oven 20 to 30 minutes or until dough is well risen and filling is tender. Cool on a wire rack. Brush with plum jam and sprinkle with flaked almonds. Makes 12 servings.

PASTRY DESSERTS

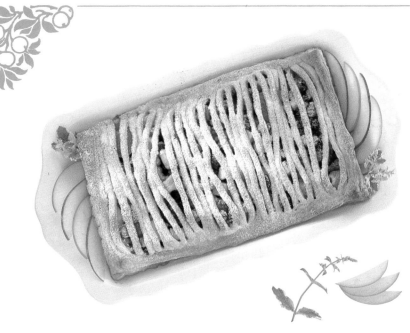

Mincemeat Jalousie

2/3 (17-1/4-oz.) package frozen puff pastry, thawed
1 tablespoon milk
1 tablespoon superfine sugar
Apple slices and fresh herbs to garnish, if desired
Whipped cream to serve, if desired

Mincemeat:
2 eating apples
2 bananas
Juice and grated peel of 1/2 lemon and 1 orange
1/3 cup grapes
2/3 cup currants
1/2 cup golden raisins
1/2 cup dark raisins
1/4 cup almonds, coarsely chopped
1/3 cup walnuts, coarsely chopped
1/3 cup sugar
2 tablespoons brandy
3 tablespoons butter, melted

To prepare mincemeat, peel, core and chop apples. Peel and chop bananas. In a large bowl, quickly toss prepared fruit in lemon juice. Halve and seed grapes and add to fruit with orange juice and lemon and orange peels. Add currants and raisins. Add chopped nuts, sugar and brandy to mixture and mix well. Stir in melted butter.

Dampen a baking sheet. Roll out pastry to a 12" x 5" rectangle. Cut in half.

Place 1 pastry half on dampened baking sheet and spread about 1/2 of mincemeat on top to within 1 inch of edges. Reserve remaining mincemeat for another use. Moisten edges with water. Roll out remaining pastry half 1 inch larger all around than other piece. Fold in half lengthwise and make cuts down from folded edge, 1/2 inch apart to within 1 inch of edge. Open and lifting carefully, place over mincemeat and pastry.

Press edges of pastry together and flute edges. Chill jalousie 30 minutes. Preheat oven to 425F (220C). Brush jalousie lightly with milk and sprinkle with sugar. Bake 30 to 35 minutes, until pastry is puffed up and golden.

If pastry starts to brown too quickly, cover with foil. Garnish with apple slices and fresh herbs, if desired. Serve with whipped cream, if desired.

Makes 6 servings.

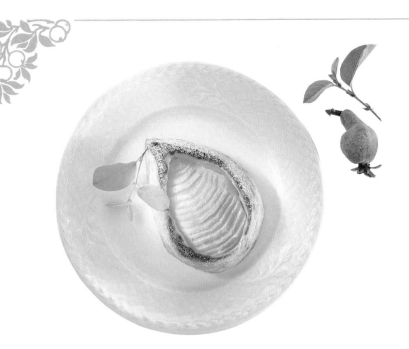

Individual Pear Puffs

8 ounces fresh or frozen puff pastry
2 large ripe pears
1 egg yolk
1 tablespoon milk
Superfine sugar
Fresh herbs to garnish, if desired
Poire William liqueur, if desired

Preheat oven to 425F (220C). Thaw pastry, if frozen, and roll out to a rectangle about 1/4 inch thick. Using half a pear as a guide, cut out pastry pear shapes 1/2 inch larger than pears, then cut around pear leaving a pear-shaped frame.

Roll out solid pear shape to same size as frame, dampen edges with water and fit frame on top. Press edges together lightly. Prepare 3 more pastry pear shapes in same way. Peel and halve pears. Core pears and cut crosswise in thin slices. Place in pastry shapes.

Place pear puffs on a baking sheet. In a small bowl, beat egg yolk and milk and brush edges of pastry. Bake 15 to 20 minutes, until pears are tender and pastry edges are puffed up and golden. Remove from oven, sprinkle with sugar and broil 1 minute. Transfer to serving plates. Garnish with fresh herbs, if desired. If desired, heat liqueur in a small saucepan, light and pour flaming over puffs. Serve at once.

Makes 4 servings.

Strawberry Mille-Feuille

13 ounces fresh or frozen puff pastry
1 pound strawberries
1-1/4 cups whipping cream
1 to 2 drops vanilla extract
Sugar to taste
1/4 cup plus 1 tablespoon red currant jelly
2 tablespoons water

Thaw pastry, if frozen. Preheat oven to 425F (220C). Roll out pastry to a thin rectangle and cut in 3 equal sections.

Place sections on baking sheets and prick all over with a fork. Bake 15 to 20 minutes, until golden-brown and crisp. Cool on a wire rack. When cold, trim edges with a very sharp knife to make even. Reserve trimmings. Cut 1/2 of strawberries in half, using even-sized ones. Slice remainder. In a bowl, whip cream until fairly stiff and flavor with vanilla and sugar. Fold sliced strawberries into whipped cream.

Place 1 pastry slice on a serving plate and spread with 1/2 of whipped cream mixture. Lay another slice on top and spread with remaining cream mixture. Top with remaining slice. In a small saucepan, heat jelly and water gently until jelly has dissolved. Brush top slice with jelly and arrange halved strawberries on top. Brush with remainder of jelly. Crush reserved pastry trimmings and press into sides of mille-feuille.

Makes 6 to 8 servings.

Tarte Francaise

13 ounces fresh or frozen puff pastry
1 egg yolk, beaten
1/4 cup plus 2 tablespoons apricot jam, sieved
2 tablespoons lemon juice
1-1/2 pounds mixed fresh fruit such as grapes, strawberries, raspberries and bananas
Additional strawberries and leaves to garnish, if desired

Thaw pastry, if frozen, and roll out to a 12" x 8" rectangle. Fold pastry in half. Cut a rectangle from folded edge 1-1/2 inches in from outside edges.

Unfold middle section and roll out to a 12" x 8" rectangle. Place on a baking sheet, dampen edges with water, then unfold frame and place carefully on top of pastry rectangle. Press edges of pastry together. Mark a pattern on frame and brush with beaten egg yolk. Prick center all over.

Preheat oven to 425F (220C). Chill pastry 10 minutes, then bake about 20 minutes, until golden-brown; cool. In a saucepan, heat jam and lemon juice gently until jam has melted. Halve and seed grapes. Leave strawberries and raspberries whole and peel and slice bananas. Brush bottom of tart lightly with jam and arrange prepared fruit in rows. Brush fruit with jam and garnish with additional strawberries and leaves, if desired. Serve as soon as possible.

Makes 6 servings.

Kumquat & Cranberry Tarts

3/4 cup superfine sugar
1 cup water
8 oz. kumquats, sliced
1-1/2 cups cranberries
2 (3-oz.) pkgs. cream cheese, softened
1/3 cup plain yogurt
1 teaspoon arrowroot

Walnut Pastry:
1-1/2 cups all-purpose flour
1/2 cup butter
1/2 cup chopped walnuts
1/4 cup superfine sugar
1 egg, beaten

To prepare pastry, sift flour into a bowl. Cut butter into flour finely until mixture resembles fine bread crumbs. Stir in walnuts, sugar and egg. With a fork, mix to form a soft dough.

Knead on a lightly floured surface. Roll out and line 6 (4-1/2-inch) fluted flan pans. Trim edges, prick bottom and chill 30 minutes. Preheat oven to 375F (190C). Gently heat sugar and water in a saucepan until dissolved. Bring to a boil. Add kumquats and cook 3 minutes or until tender. Strain into a sieve. Return 1/3 of syrup to pan; reserve remaining syrup. Add cranberries to syrup in saucepan. Bring to a boil, cover and cook 3 minutes or until tender. Strain into a sieve. Keep syrups and fruits separate. Bake pastries 10 to 15 minutes or until lightly browned. Let stand until cold.

In a bowl, beat cream cheese and yogurt. Spread over bottom of pastries. Arrange alternate circles of kumquats and cranberries on cream cheese mixture. Blend 1/2 teaspoon of arrowroot into each syrup and bring each to a boil separately. Glaze kumquats with clear syrup and cranberries with red syrup. Let stand until set. Makes 8 servings.

Golden Cream Flan

Shortcrust Pastry:
2 cups all-purpose flour
Pinch of salt
8 tablespoons butter, cut in cubes
1 teaspoon sugar, if desired
2 to 3 tablespoons chilled water or milk

Filling:
1/2 cup corn syrup
3 tablespoons butter, cut in cubes
1/4 cup dairy sour cream
Grated peel of 1 lemon
2 eggs, beaten

Lemon slices and fresh herbs to garnish, if
**   desired**
Whipped cream to serve, if desired

Sift flour and salt into a large bowl and add butter. Using fingertips, cut butter into flour until mixture resembles bread crumbs.

Stir in sugar, if desired. Stir in enough water or milk to make a firm but not sticky dough. Knead lightly on a floured surface. Wrap pastry in foil and chill 30 minutes; this allows flour to expand and helps to prevent pastry shrinking during baking. Meanwhile, preheat oven to 375F (190C).

Roll out pastry 1 inch larger than an 8-inch flan pan. Using a rolling pin, lift pastry and lower into flan pan. Press gently into sides and trim off any excess with a sharp knife.

To bake blind, fold foil in 1-inch strips, using several thicknesses, and press around sides. Prick bottom and bake 15 to 20 minutes, until dry and lightly colored.

To prepare filling, in a medium-size saucepan, warm corn syrup over low heat. Remove from heat and add butter. Stir until butter has melted. Stir in sour cream and lemon peel. Whisk eggs into mixture, until thoroughly incorporated. Pour mixture in pastry shell.

Bake 45 to 55 minutes, until filling is golden-brown and puffed up. Garnish with lemon slices and fresh herbs, if desired. Serve warm or cold with whipped cream, if desired.

Makes 6 servings.

Pecan Pie

1 recipe Shortcrust Pastry, page 77
3 eggs
2 cups packed light-brown sugar
1 tablespoon honey
2 tablespoons butter, melted
2 tablespoons whipping cream
Pinch of salt
1-1/2 cups pecans, coarsely chopped
Powdered sugar

Prepare pastry as directed and line a 10-inch flan pan. Bake blind as directed on page 77. Leave oven temperature at 375F (190C).

In a large bowl, whisk eggs and brown sugar until pale and thick. Stir in honey, butter, whipping cream and salt and mix thoroughly. Fold in chopped pecans.

Pour mixture evenly into baked pastry shell and bake 20 minutes. Lower oven temperature to 325F (165C) and bake 45 to 50 minutes more, until set. Dust with powdered sugar and serve warm or chilled.

Makes 6 servings.

VARIATION: Substitute walnuts for pecans, if desired.

Orange Meringue Pie

1 recipe Shortcrust Pastry, page 77
1/4 cup cornstarch
1-1/4 cups water
2 tablespoons butter
Grated peel and juice of 2 small oranges
Juice of 1 small lime
2 eggs, separated
3/4 cup superfine sugar
Orange and lime twists and mint leaves to garnish, if desired

Preheat oven to 375F (190C). Prepare pastry as directed and line a 10-inch flan pan. Bake blind as directed on page 77. Lower oven temperature to 325F (165C).

In a bowl, mix cornstarch and a small amount of water to a smooth paste. Stir in remaining water, then pour into a saucepan and add butter. Bring to a boil, stirring constantly. Simmer 2 to 3 minutes, stirring constantly, and remove from heat. Beat in citrus juices and grated orange peel, egg yolks and 1/3 of sugar. Spoon into baked pastry shell and cool slightly.

In a large bowl, whisk egg whites until stiff but not dry. Add 1/2 of remaining sugar and whisk again until mixture holds its shape. Fold in remaining sugar. Using a pastry bag fitted with a star nozzle, pipe meringue on top of flan to cover filling and pastry. Bake 2 to 3 minutes, until meringue is set and lightly golden. Serve warm or cold, garnished with orange and lime twists and mint leaves, if desired.

Makes 6 to 8 servings.

Clementine Tartlets

1 recipe Shortcrust Pastry, page 77
Juice of 2 oranges and 1 lemon
2-1/4 cups superfine sugar
4 clementines
2 eggs plus 2 extra yolks
8 tablespoons butter, softened
1 tablespoon ground almonds
2 or 3 tablespoons Grand Marnier or Cointreau

Prepare pastry as directed and line 6 (5-inch) tartlet pans. Bake blind 10 to 15 minutes as directed on page 77. Leave oven temperature at 375F (190C).

In a saucepan, combine orange and lemon juices and 1-1/4 cups of sugar. Cook over medium heat until sugar has dissolved, then boil syrup 15 minutes. Peel clementines and cut in slices. Cut slices in half and add to syrup. Simmer gently 2 to 3 minutes. Using a slotted spoon, transfer clementines to a plate and boil syrup until very thick and syrupy. Set aside. In a bowl, beat eggs, extra yolks and remaining sugar until well mixed. Beat in butter, ground almonds and liqueur.

Divide mixture among baked pastry shells and bake about 8 minutes, until set and golden; cool. When cold, brush top of tartlets with thick syrup and arrange clementine slices on top. Brush with more syrup, then chill.

Makes 6 servings.

VARIATION: Use strawberries or blackberries instead of clementines, but immerse in syrup only for a few seconds.

Chocolate Profiteroles

Choux Pastry
4 tablespoons butter, cut in small pieces
2/3 cup water
1/2 cup plus 2 tablespoons all-purpose flour, sifted
2 eggs, beaten
1-1/4 cups whipping cream
1 recipe Dark Chocolate Sauce, page 92

Preheat oven to 400F (205C). Line several baking sheets with parchment paper. To prepare choux pastry, combine butter and water in a saucepan and cook over medium heat until butter melts. Bring to a boil and remove from heat. Add flour and beat with a wooden spoon until mixture leaves sides of pan.

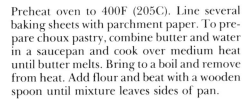

Beat in eggs gradually, until mixture is smooth and shiny. Using a pastry bag fitted with a plain nozzle, pipe walnut-size balls onto prepared baking sheets. Bake 20 to 25 minutes, until brown, puffed up and just crisp on outside. Make a small hole in side of each profiterole to allow steam to escape and keep profiterole crisp.

Cool profiteroles on a wire rack. To serve, whip cream until stiff. Enlarge hole in side of each profiterole and, using a pastry bag fitted with a plain nozzle, pipe cream into them. Prepare Dark Chocolate Sauce as directed. To serve, pour hot sauce over profiteroles.

Makes 4 servings.

Salambos

1 recipe Choux Pastry, page 79
1/2 cup chopped mixed nuts
3/4 cup superfine sugar
5 or 6 sugar lumps
1 medium-sized orange
1-1/4 cups whipping cream
Shredded orange peel to garnish, if desired

Prepare choux pastry as directed and bake as for profiteroles, page 79. Brown nuts in an ovenproof dish at same time, turning occasionally to brown evenly; cool.

In a heavy-bottom saucepan, melt superfine sugar over very low heat. Cook to a golden-brown caramel. Quickly dip each choux puff into caramel and then into nuts, coating puffs quite thickly. Let stand until caramel hardens.

Rub sugar lumps over orange peel to remove oil. Place lumps in a bowl, squeeze orange and add juice to lumps. Crush lumps with a wooden spoon. In a separate bowl, whip cream until fairly stiff, then whisk in orange juice and sugar until cream is thick. Using a pastry bag fitted with a plain nozzle, pipe cream into choux puffs. Serve within 1 hour, garnished with shredded orange peel, if desired.

Makes 4 servings.

Beignets

1 recipe Raspberry Sauce, page 91, Mincemeat Sauce, page 92 or Hot Lemon Sauce, page 93
1 recipe Choux Pastry, page 79
Vegetable oil for deep-frying
Superfine sugar
Fresh herbs to garnish, if desired

Prepare Raspberry Sauce, Mincemeat Sauce or Hot Lemon Sauce as directed. Prepare choux pastry as directed, but set aside after adding eggs. Heat oil for deep frying to 355F (180C).

Drop teaspoonfuls of pastry into oil. As beignets swell, increase heat so temperature of oil rises to 375F (190C) (see note below). Cook until puffed up and golden all over. Drain well on paper towels and keep warm while cooking remainder.

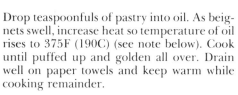

Toss warm beignets in superfine sugar to coat lightly and serve with sauce. Garnish with fresh herbs, if desired.

Makes 4 servings.

NOTE: Oil should not be at its hottest when beginning cooking beignets, or they will swell too quickly and the inside will not be done.

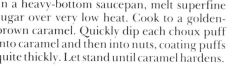

Autumn Fruit-Filled Pastry

1 recipe Choux Pastry, page 79
2 tablespoons butter
1 pound baking apples
8 ounces fresh or frozen blackberries, thawed if frozen
2 tablespoons light-brown sugar
1-1/4 cups whipping cream
Powdered sugar

Preheat oven to 425F (220C). Line a baking sheet with parchment paper. Prepare choux pastry as directed. Drop small teaspoonfuls of pastry onto prepared baking sheet in a 10-inch circle.

Bake pastry 25 to 35 minutes, until puffed up and golden. Split circle in half horizontally; scoop out and discard any uncooked pastry. Place halves cut side up on baking sheet and return to oven 5 minutes; cool. In a saucepan, melt butter. Peel, core and slice apples. Add sliced apples, blackberries and brown sugar to butter. Cover and simmer gently until fruit is soft but not pulpy. Remove from heat and cool.

Place bottom half of pastry on a serving dish. Whip cream until stiff and spoon into pastry. Reserve a small amount of fruit for garnish. Spoon remaining fruit mixture over whipped cream and top with remaining pastry. Dust with powdered sugar and garnish with reserved fruit. Serve immediately.

Makes 4 servings.

NOTE: Pastry balls should just touch each other; they will connect during cooking. Do not smooth out balls, the finished effect will be slightly rough.

Apricot & Hazelnut Galette

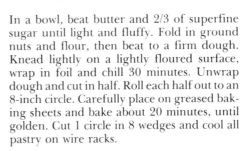

1/2 cup hazelnuts, skins removed
1/3 cup butter, softened
1/3 cup superfine sugar
1 cup all-purpose flour
8 ounces fresh apricots, halved, pitted
3 tablespoons water
1-1/4 cups whipping cream
Powdered sugar
Additional toasted hazelnuts and apricot slices to garnish, if desired.

Toast hazelnuts under broiler to brown evenly. Reserve 8 nuts and grind remainder finely in a coffee grinder. Preheat oven to 350F (175C). Lightly grease 2 baking sheets.

In a bowl, beat butter and 2/3 of superfine sugar until light and fluffy. Fold in ground nuts and flour, then beat to a firm dough. Knead lightly on a lightly floured surface, wrap in foil and chill 30 minutes. Unwrap dough and cut in half. Roll each half out to an 8-inch circle. Carefully place on greased baking sheets and bake about 20 minutes, until golden. Cut 1 circle in 8 wedges and cool all pastry on wire racks.

Poach apricots and remaining superfine sugar gently in water, until just soft; cool. In a bowl, whip cream until stiff. Transfer pastry circle to a serving plate and spread with 1/2 of whipped cream. Remove apricots from pan with a slotted spoon and arrange over whipped cream. Top with pastry wedges and dust lightly with powdered sugar. Using a pastry tube fitted with a star nozzle, pipe a rosette of remaining whipped cream onto each wedge and decorate with hazelnuts. Serve within 1 hour, garnished with additional hazelnuts and apricot slices, if desired.

Makes 8 servings.

Cream Cheese Strudel

3/4 cup chopped hazelnuts
1 (8-oz.) package cream cheese, softened
2 tablespoons superfine sugar
1 egg
Grated peel of 1 lemon
5 sheets filo pastry, thawed if frozen
4 tablespoons butter, melted
1 recipe Black Currant & Cassis sauce,
    page 90
Black currants and mint leaves to garnish, if
    desired

Preheat oven to 400F (205C). Generously grease a baking sheet. Toast hazelnuts to brown evenly; cool.

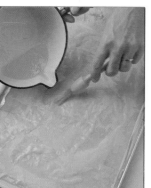

In a bowl, beat cream cheese, sugar, egg and lemon peel until smooth. Beat in toasted hazelnuts. Place 1 sheet of pastry on greased baking sheet, keeping remainder covered with a damp tea towel. Brush with melted butter and place another sheet on top. Layer all 5 sheets of pastry, brushing each one with melted butter.

Spoon cream cheese mixture in a line down center of pastry and fold either short end over filling. Roll up pastry around filling and turn over on baking sheet, so seam is underneath. Brush top of strudel with remaining butter and bake 25 to 30 minutes, until golden-brown and flaky. Meanwhile, prepare Black Currant & Cassis Sauce as directed. Serve strudel warm, cut in diagonal slices, with sauce. Garnish with black currants and mint leaves, if desired.

Makes 4 to 6 servings.

Nectarine Baklava

10 sheets filo pastry, thawed if frozen
2/3 cup butter, melted
1-3/4 cups chopped mixed nuts
1-1/2 teaspoons ground cinnamon
1/2 cup superfine sugar
Grated peel and juice of 2 lemons
1 tablespoon orange flower water
4 nectarines
Powdered sugar
Nectarine slices and fresh herbs to garnish, if
    desired

Preheat oven to 350F (175C). Cut pastry sheets in half, then cut each half in quarters.

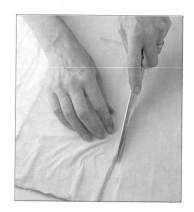

Working quickly, brush 1 cut sheet of pastry with melted butter. Line 8 individual 4-inch pans with 1 piece of pastry. Brush 3 more cut sheets with butter and lay cut pieces into pans, overlapping each other at different angles. In a bowl, combine nuts, cinnamon and 1/2 of sugar; spread 1/2 of nut mixture over pastry. Cover with 2 more layers of pastry, each brushed with butter, then top with remaining nut mixture. Cover with remaining pastry, brushed with butter.

Press down pastry in pans and bake 20 to 25 minutes, until golden-brown. Meanwhile, in a saucepan, combine remaining sugar and lemon juice. Cook, over low heat, until sugar dissolves. Stir in lemon peel and orange flower water. Bring to a boil and simmer 3 minutes; cool slightly. Slice nectarines into syrup, turning carefully to coat. Spoon into center of pastries and dust edges with powdered sugar. Serve lukewarm or cold, when pastries have absorbed some syrup. Garnish with nectarine slices and fresh herbs, if desired.

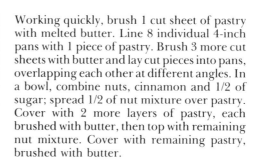

Makes 8 servings.

ICED DESSERTS

Nutty-Crumb Cream

1/2 cup hazelnuts
1-1/4 cups fresh whole-wheat bread crumbs
2 tablespoons light-brown sugar
2 egg whites
1/3 cup superfine sugar
1-1/4 cups whipping cream
1 to 2 drops vanilla extract
Fresh flower buds or leaves to decorate, if
   desired

Toast hazelnuts under broiler evenly. Cool,
then grind coarsely in a coffee grinder or a
food processor fitted with the metal blade. In
a bowl, mix ground nuts with bread crumbs
and brown sugar.

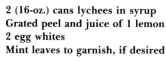

Spread crumb mixture evenly on a baking
sheet. Broil, turning and shaking, until
brown; cool. Whisk egg whites in a large bowl,
until stiff. Sprinkle in sugar and whisk 2 minutes more. Whip cream and vanilla to soft
peaks, then fold into egg whites with all but 1
tablespoon of browned crumb mixture.

Spoon mixture into 6 dessert dishes and chill
until ready to serve. Sprinkle with reserved
crumb mixture just before serving. Decorate
with fresh flower buds or leaves, if desired.

Makes 6 servings.

NOTE: This mixture makes a delicious ice
cream. Pour finished cream into a plastic container and freeze.

Lychee Sorbet

2 (16-oz.) cans lychees in syrup
Grated peel and juice of 1 lemon
2 egg whites
Mint leaves to garnish, if desired

Drain lychees, reserving 1-1/4 cups of syrup.
In a blender or food processor fitted with the
metal blade, process lychees, syrup and
lemon juice to a puree.

Stir in lemon peel, pour into a plastic container and freeze about 1 hour, until mixture
is slushy.

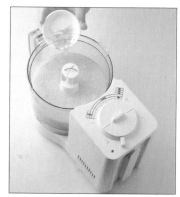

In a large bowl, whisk egg whites until stiff.
Fold in semifrozen lychee puree and combine
thoroughly. Freeze until firm. To serve,
scoop sorbet in balls and garnish with mint
leaves, if desired.

Makes 4 to 6 servings.

NOTE: For a smoother texture, whisk sorbet
about 1 hour after adding egg whites. Serve
sorbet as soon as possible for the best flavor.

Mandarin Fig Sorbet

1/2 cup superfine sugar
2/3 cup plus 3 tablespoons water
Peel and juice 4 mandarins
6 green figs
2 teaspoons plain gelatin
2 egg whites
Mandarin shell halves, if desired
Fig slices and mint sprigs to decorate

In a saucepan, heat sugar and 2/3 cup of water, stirring occasionally, until dissolved. Add mandarin peel and figs. Bring to a boil, cover and simmer 10 minutes. Let stand until cold.

Remove mandarin peel. Pour remaining liquid and figs into a food processor fitted with a metal blade. Process to a purée. Sieve mixture into a bowl. In a small bowl, sprinkle gelatin over 3 tablespoons of water and let stand to soften 2 to 3 minutes. Stand bowl in a saucepan of hot water and stir until dissolved and quite hot. Add gelatin and mandarin juice to fig purée; stir until well blended. Pour into a plastic container. Cover and freeze 2 hours or until partially frozen but still soft.

Spoon mixture into food processor and process until creamy, well blended and smooth. In a bowl, whisk egg whites until stiff. Fold in fig purée mixture until smooth. Return mixture to container. Cover and freeze until firm or until needed. Soften 15 minutes before serving in scoops. Serve in mandarin shell halves, if desired. Decorate with fresh fig slices and mint sprigs. Makes 6 servings.

Amaretti Meringue Bombes

1 tablespoon butter, melted
20 Amaretti cookies (macaroons), crushed finely
12 oz. raspberries, thawed if frozen
1 tablespoon plus 1 teaspoon powdered sugar
Additional raspberries and mint sprigs to decorate
Amaretti cookies (macaroons), if desired

Filling:
2 cups coarsely crushed meringues
2-1/2 cups whipping cream
1/4 cup Amaretti cookies (macaroons), broken in small pieces
1/4 cup maraschino cherries, chopped
1/4 cup chocolate morsels

Brush insides of 8 tiny molds with melted butter. Divide crushed cookies among molds and shake well to coat evenly. Chill.

To prepare filling, mix meringues, cookie pieces, cherries and chocolate in a bowl. Stir to mix well. In another bowl, whip cream to soft peaks. Add meringue mixture to whipped cream and fold in very gently until evenly mixed. Fill each mold with meringue mixture, pressing down to pack evenly. Cover and freeze until needed. In a food processor fitted with a metal blade, process raspberries and powdered sugar to a purée. Sieve raspberry purée into a bowl.

Just before serving, dip each mold into hand-hot water and invert onto serving plates. Decorate with raspberries and mint sprigs. Serve with raspberry purée and cookies, if desired. Makes 8 servings.

Coffee Bombe

1/2 recipe of Meringues, page 30
3 eggs, separated
3/4 cup superfine sugar
1-1/3 cups cold strong coffee
2 cups whipping cream
1 recipe Bitter Mocha Sauce, page 93, to serve
Whipped cream and chocolate coffee beans to
    decorate, if desired

Prepare meringues as directed. Lightly oil a
4-cup bombe mold. In a large bowl, beat egg
yolks and sugar until thick and mousse-like.
Gently stir in coffee. In a separate bowl, whip
cream lightly. Crush meringues.

Fold cream and meringues into coffee mixture. In a medium-size bowl, whisk egg whites
until stiff and fold 1 tablespoon into coffee
mixture. Carefully fold coffee mixture into
egg whites. Pour into oiled mold and freeze
until firm.

One hour before serving, place bombe in refrigerator to soften slightly. Prepare Bitter
Mocha Sauce as directed. Turn out bombe
onto a serving dish and decorate with
whipped cream and chocolate coffee beans, if
desired. Serve with hot sauce.

Makes 8 servings.

NOTE: To remove bombe, immerse a tea
towel in very hot water, wring out and wrap
around mold. Invert onto a serving plate and
lift off mold.

Frozen Kiwifruit Terrine

1 recipe Passion-Fruit Mousse, page 29
6 kiwifruit
3/4 cup whipping cream

Lightly oil an 8" x 4" loaf pan. Prepare
mousse as directed and spoon 1/3 of mousse
into oiled pan. Freeze until set.

Peel kiwifruit and cut across fruit in thin
slices. Arrange 2 sliced kiwifruit over top of
mousse in rows, then carefully spoon 1/2 of
remaining mousse on top. Freeze again until
set. Repeat process with 2 more sliced kiwifruit and top with remaining mousse. Return
to freezer.

About 2 hours before serving, remove terrine
from freezer and turn out onto a serving dish.
In a bowl, whip cream until stiff. Using a
pastry bag fitted with a star nozzle, pipe a ruff
down each side of terrine. Decorate with
remaining 2 sliced kiwifruit.

Makes 6 servings.

NOTE: Select kiwifruit that give slightly
when squeezed, but are not too soft.

Frozen Loganberry Soufflé

1 pound loganberries or raspberries
Lemon juice to taste
2/3 cup superfine sugar
1/2 cup water
3 egg whites
1-3/4 cups whipping cream
Fresh raspberries and mint leaves to garnish, if
** desired**

In a blender or food processor fitted with the metal blade, process berries to a puree, then sieve to remove seeds. Flavor with lemon juice.

In a small saucepan, combine sugar and water. Cook over low heat. When sugar dissolves, bring syrup to a boil and boil to 240F (115C). In a large bowl, whisk egg whites until stiff. Gradually pour in sugar syrup, whisking constantly. Continue whisking until meringue is firm and cool. In a bowl, whip cream lightly and fold into meringue mixture with fruit puree.

Divide mixture among 6 ramekin dishes and freeze 2 to 3 hours. Transfer to refrigerator 30 minutes before serving. Garnish with fresh raspberries and mint leaves, if desired.

Makes 6 servings.

NOTE: For a special occasion, wrap foil around tops of small ramekin dishes so that foil extends 2 inches above rim. Keep in place with freezer tape. Fill dishes to come over the top, so when foil is removed, they look like risen soufflés.

Pineapple Alaska

1 large ripe pineapple with leaves
1 to 2 tablespoons kirsch
1 quart vanilla ice cream
3 egg whites
3/4 cup plus 1 tablespoon superfine sugar

Cut pineapple in half lengthwise. Using a grapefruit knife, cut out pulp. Discard core, then cut pulp in chunks and place in a bowl. Sprinkle with kirsch, cover with plastic wrap and chill pulp and pineapple shells overnight.

Place pineapple chunks in shells and pack ice cream on top. Freeze about 2 hours, until very firm. Preheat oven to 400F (205C). Whisk egg whites in a bowl until stiff. Whisk in 1/4 cup plus 2 tablespoons of sugar, then whisk 1 minute more. Fold in 1/4 cup plus 2 tablespoons of sugar.

Pile meringue over ice cream, completely covering ice cream. Make small peaks in meringue with a flat-bladed knife. Place pineapple shells on a baking sheet and sprinkle with remaining sugar. Bake about 8 minutes, until meringue is set and brown. Serve immediately.

Makes 6 servings.

VARIATION: Prepare this dessert using a fruit sorbet instead of vanilla ice cream.

Gooseberry Ice Cream

1-1/2 pounds fresh or frozen gooseberries
1/4 cup water
1/2 cup superfine sugar
3 egg yolks
1 small avocado
1-1/4 cups whipping cream
Gooseberries, fresh herbs or borage flowers to decorate, if desired

In a saucepan, combine gooseberries and 2 tablespoons of water. Cook over a low heat until gooseberries are soft. Puree in a blender or food processor, then sieve to remove seeds; cool.

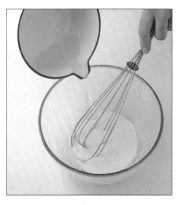

Combine remaining water and sugar in a saucepan. Dissolve over medium heat, stirring constantly, then boil syrup to thread stage 225F (105C). In a bowl, beat egg yolks lightly, then pour syrup into them and whisk until mixture is thick and mousse-like. Peel avocado, discard pit and mash pulp; mix into gooseberry puree. Whip cream and fold into egg mixture with puree. Turn into a rigid plastic container and freeze 1 to 2 hours, until beginning to firm.

Remove from freezer and beat well. Freeze until firm. Transfer to refrigerator 30 minutes before serving to soften. Serve in scoops in chilled dessert dishes. Decorate with gooseberries, fresh herbs or borage flowers, if desired.

Makes 4 to 6 servings.

NOTE: Avocado gives this ice-cream a lovely texture. Its taste is not discernible.
When cooking acidic fruits, such as gooseberries, do not use an aluminum pan, or the fruit will taste metallic.

Lychee & Port Ice Cream

1/2 cup superfine sugar
2/3 cup ruby port
20 fresh lychees or 1 (15-oz.) can lychees
1 tablespoon plus 1 teaspoon lime juice
1-1/4 cups whipping cream
Fresh or canned lychees and lime peel twists to decorate

In a saucepan, combine sugar and port. Heat gently, stirring occasionally, until sugar has dissolved. Peel lychees and remove pits or drain canned lychees. Add lychees to port mixture. Bring to a boil, cover and cook very gently 2 minutes. Let stand until completely cold.

Using a food processor fitted with a metal blade, process port and lychees until smooth. Pour mixture into a sieve set over a bowl and rub mixture through using a wooden spoon. Stir in lime juice. In a bowl, whip cream until thick. Add port mixture to whipped cream and fold in until evenly blended. Pour mixture into a plastic container, cover and freeze 1 to 2 hours or until mixture is almost frozen but still soft.

Return mixture to food processor. Process until smooth and creamy. Return mixture to plastic container and freeze until firm. Scoop ice cream to serve. Decorate with lychees and lime peel. Makes 6 servings.

SAUCES &
ACCOMPANIMENTS

Black Currant & Cassis Sauce

8 ounces fresh or frozen black currants
1/4 cup superfine sugar
1/2 cup water
2 tablespoons crème de cassis

In a saucepan, combine black currants, sugar and water. Cook over medium heat until currants are juicy and tender.

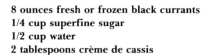

Drain currants, reserving juice. Push currants through a sieve with a little juice to make a puree. Stir in liqueur and enough juice to desired consistency. Serve cold, if desired.

Makes 4 to 6 servings.

NOTE: Serve with Coeurs à la Crème, page 16, if desired.

Mousseline Sauce

1 egg plus 1 extra yolk
2 tablespoons plus 2 teaspoons superfine sugar
2 tablespoons cream sherry

Combine all ingredients in top of a double boiler or a bowl set over a pan of simmering water.

Using a whisk, whisk ingredients until very thick and foamy, about 10 minutes.

Makes 4 servings.

NOTE: Serve with Caramel Fruit Kabobs, page 46, if desired.

Crème à la Vanille

1-1/4 cups milk
1 vanilla bean
2 large egg yolks
1 tablespoon superfine sugar
1 teaspoon cornstarch or arrowroot

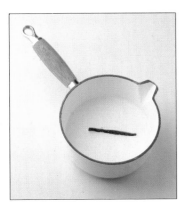

Place milk and vanilla bean in a saucepan. Bring almost to boiling point, then remove from heat. Cover and let stand 5 to 10 minutes to infuse.

In a bowl, beat egg yolks, sugar and cornstarch or arrowroot. Remove vanilla bean, then pour hot milk onto egg mixture, stirring constantly.

Return to clean pan and heat gently without boiling, stirring constantly, until sauce has thickened sufficiently to coat back of a spoon. Strain and serve hot or cold.

Makes 4 servings.

NOTE: Serve with Bread & Fruit Pudding, page 18, if desired.

Raspberry Sauce

1-3/4 cups fresh or frozen raspberries
2 tablespoons lemon juice
1/4 to 1/3 cup superfine sugar
1/3 cup framboise liqueur or water

Combine all ingredients in a saucepan and bring slowly to a boil.

Simmer a few minutes. Serve immediately or, using a wooden spoon, press through a nylon sieve and serve cold.

Makes 4 to 6 servings.

NOTE: Serve with Orange Roll, page 71, if desired.

Mincemeat Sauce

2 eating apples
2 small bananas
Grated peel and juice of 1 lemon
6 ounces grapes
1 tablespoon plus 1-1/2 teaspoons butter
1/3 cup sliced almonds
2 tablespoons black currants
2 tablespoons golden raisins
Rum or brandy to taste

Peel, core and finely dice apples. Peel and finely dice bananas. Sprinkle with some of lemon juice.

Halve and seed grapes. In a saucepan, melt butter and saute almonds over medium heat until turning brown. Add prepared fruits and remaining lemon juice, lemon peel, currants and raisins.

Stir over heat a few minutes, then flavor with rum or brandy. Serve hot.

Makes 4 to 6 servings.

VARIATION: Add brown sugar to taste.

NOTE: Serve with Vanilla Bavarois, page 11 if desired.

Dark Chocolate Sauce

6 ounces semisweet chocolate
1/2 cup strong coffee or water
1/4 cup superfine sugar

Break chocolate in pieces and put into top of a double boiler or a bowl set over a pan of simmering water. Add coffee or water and sugar.

Stir over medium heat until chocolate melts and sauce is smooth and creamy. Serve hot or cold.

Makes 4 to 6 servings.

NOTE: Serve with White Dark Chocolate Terrine, page 62, if desired.

Bitter Mocha Sauce

3 ounces semisweet chocolate
1 tablespoon dark very strong coarsely ground
**   expresso coffee**
1-1/4 cups whipping cream
1-1/2 teaspoons butter

Break chocolate in small pieces and place in top of a double boiler or a bowl. In a saucepan, combine coffee and whipping cream. Bring to a boil and remove from heat. Let stand 30 minutes to infuse.

Strain creamy coffee through a fine sieve into chocolate. Place over a pan of simmering water and stir until chocolate melts.

Whisk in butter to make sauce glossy and serve at once.

Makes 6 to 8 servings.

NOTE: Serve with Coffee Bombe, page 86 if desired.

Hot Lemon Sauce

Grated peel and juice of 3 lemons
1/3 cup butter
1/3 cup superfine sugar
1 teaspoon cornstarch
Water

In a saucepan, combine lemon peel and juice, butter and sugar. Stir over gentle heat until butter melts and sugar dissolves.

Mix cornstarch and a small amount of water to a smooth paste; stir into lemon mixture. Bring sauce to a boil, stirring constantly.

Simmer 1 to 2 minutes, stirring constantly. Keep warm until ready to serve.

Makes 4 to 6 servings.

NOTE: Serve with Austrian Cheesecake, page 21, if desired.

Chocolate Cigarettes

2 egg whites
1/3 cup plus 1 tablespoon superfine sugar
1/4 cup plus 3 tablespoons all-purpose flour
2 teaspoons cocoa powder
1/4 cup unsalted butter, melted
2 (1-oz.) squares white chocolate, melted
Holly sprigs to decorate

Preheat oven to 400F (205C). Line 2 baking sheets with waxed paper. In a bowl, whisk egg whites until stiff. Add sugar gradually, whisking well after each addition. Sift flour and cocoa over surface of mixture. Add butter and fold in carefully until mixture is evenly blended.

Place 2 spoonfuls of mixture onto each prepared baking sheet, spacing well apart. Spread each in a thin round. Bake 1 sheet at a time in oven 3 to 4 minutes. Loosen each round with a palette knife, then return to oven 1 minute.

Remove 1 chocolate round at a time and quickly roll around a greased pencil or wooden spoon handle to form a tube. Slip off and cool cigarette on a wire rack. Repeat with remaining rounds. Cook second tray of rounds, then repeat to make cigarettes. Dip both ends of each cigarette into melted chocolate. Let set on waxed paper-lined baking sheet. Store in an airtight container until needed. Decorate with holly sprigs. Makes 25 pieces.

Creme de Menthe Cookies

8 (1-oz.) squares semi-sweet chocolate
2 tablespoons butter
2 cups graham cracker crumbs
3/4 cup plain cake crumbs
Superfine sugar
Mint sprigs to decorate

Filling:
1/4 cup unsalted butter
3/4 cup powdered sugar, sieved
2 teaspoons Creme de Menthe

To prepare filling, beat butter in a bowl with a wooden spoon or electric mixer until soft and smooth. Gradually beat in powdered sugar and Creme de Menthe until light and fluffy.

Break up chocolate and place in a bowl with butter over a saucepan of hand-hot water. Stir occasionally until melted. Add graham cracker and cake crumbs; stir until evenly mixed and mixture forms a ball. Sprinkle a 10-inch square of foil with superfine sugar.

Roll out chocolate mixture on foil in an 8-inch square. Spread filling evenly over chocolate mixture to within 1/2 inch of edges. Roll up carefully from long edge in a smooth roll using foil. Wrap in foil and chill until firm. Cut in thin slices when needed. Decorate with mint sprigs. Makes 20 servings.

Tiny Chocolate Logs

3 eggs
2 tablespoons plus 2 teaspoons superfine sugar
1/4 cup all-purpose flour
1 tablespoon cocoa powder
Powdered sugar, if desired
Marzipan toadstools and holly sprigs to decorate

Filling:
1-1/4 cups whipping cream
4 (1-oz.) squares semisweet chocolate

Preheat oven to 400F (205C). Line a 1-inch deep 12-inch baking sheet with waxed paper. Place eggs and sugar in a bowl set over a saucepan of simmering water. Whisk until thick and pale.

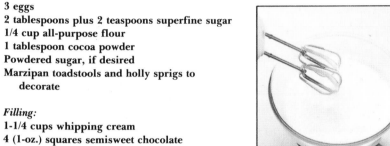

Remove bowl from saucepan; continue whisking until mixture leaves a trail when whisk is lifted. Sift flour and cocoa onto surface of mixture; fold in carefully until mixture is evenly blended. Pour mixture onto prepared baking sheet; spread carefully to edges. Bake in oven 8 to 10 minutes or until firm to touch. Cool a few minutes and remove cake. Remove waxed paper, trim edges and cut cake in half. To prepare filling, place 1/4 cup whipping cream and chocolate broken into pieces in a bowl set over saucepan of hot water. Stir occasionally until melted. Whip remaining cream until almost thick.

When chocolate has cooled, fold it carefully into whipped cream. Using 1/3 of chocolate cream, spread evenly over each cake. Roll each in a firm roll from long edge. Wrap in plastic wrap and chill 20 minutes or until firm. Cut each roll in 6 lengths. Spread each with remaining chocolate cream using a small palette knife; mark cream in lines. Sprinkle with powdered sugar, if desired. Decorate with toadstools and holly. Refrigerate until ready to serve. Makes 12 servings.

Brandy Butter

1 cup unsalted butter
1 cup superfine sugar
1/3 cup brandy
Holly sprig to decorate

In a bowl or food processor fitted with a metal blade, beat or process butter until white and creamy. Add sugar and beat or process until light and fluffy.

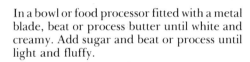

Add brandy a drop at a time, beating continuously, until enough has been added to well-flavor butter. Take care mixture does not curdle through overbeating.

Spoon butter into a glass dish and serve with a spoon or spread about 1/2 inch thick over a flat dish and chill until hard. Using a fancy cutter, cut in shapes and arrange on a chilled serving dish. Decorate with holly. Makes 8 servings.

INDEX